Wildflower Designs for Needlework

Charts, Histories and Watercolors of 29 Wildflowers

Adalee Winter

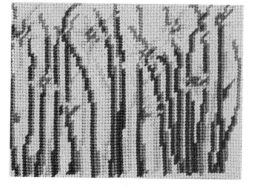

Oxmoor House®

Contents

Introduction...6
Silky and Mountain Camellia 9
Carolina Pink 10
Lupine..10
Fire Pink...11
Indian Strawberry 12
Wild Azalea...13
Yellow Jessamine...14
Wild Man of the Earth 14
Prickly Pear Cactus 16
Purple Joe-Pye Weed 17
Tickseed Coreopsis 18
Red Clover...19
Queen Anne's Lace 20
Sundrops...21
Blue-Eyed Grass..21
Passion Flower 22
Dwarf Crested Iris 22
Purple Trillium 24
Tall Goldenrod 25
Flowering Dogwood..26
Sweet Bay..27
Wild Ginger 27
Orange Milkwort 28
Dayflower 29
Violet 30
Butterflyweed 32
Charts 33
Making a Rug..73
Working from a Charted Design 75
Working Cross Stitch and Needlepoint 77
Blocking Needlework 78
Choosing Colors and Materials 79
Bibliography...80

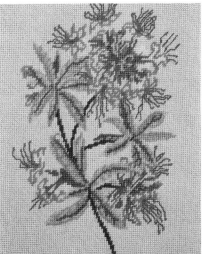

Introduction

Wildflowers are friends of my childhood. I remember my delight as the first blossoms would appear in the early spring, and my disappointment as the last colors faded for winter. The sprays of white dogwood were particular favorites when I lived on a farm. And I could pass hours lying on my back in fields of fragrant clover watching clouds change shape. During those depression years, we didn't have many "store bought" toys, so we made toys of things that were available to us. The little brown jug-shaped flowers of the Wild Ginger plant became tea cups for my dolls. I made deeply colored, but barely scented, "perfume" from wild morning glories. I blew the white fluff from the seedball of the dandelion, knowing that if I blew it all away with one breath, my wish would come true.

My mother planted her flower garden by broadcasting seed over the turned ground so that they grew as informally as do wildflowers in the field. But after my family moved to town, the flowers we lived with were almost always planted in neat rows or beds, or bought from the florist.

Many years later I became intrigued with the masses of flowers I saw growing along the highways. I was often fortunate to have a good friend traveling with me who knew and loved wildflowers from hiking in the mountains. When I asked what a particular flower was, she could tell me not only the name, but also a story about it.

During those years my husband bought 20 acres of land outside of town that included a fishing pond, marsh, pine woods, and open fields. I didn't have the patience to fish, but enjoyed exploring the property instead. In six weeks I found over *fifty* types of wildflowers. I began taking a notebook and watercolors with me on our family excursions. I spent many happy hours sitting in sand, dirt, fallen leaves, or mud, painting the flowers I found and writing down as many things as I could notice about the plants.

Looking through the pages of my notebook helps me to recall many happy times with my parents, my husband, and our children. When we moved from South Carolina (where I expected and hoped to spend the rest of my life) to Alabama, I was devastated. But on the long slope that leads to the lake at the back of our house I found not only my familiar wildflowers, but many new ones as well!

In addition to appreciating their beauty, I enjoy learning the names of the flowers and the origins of those names, both botanical and common, and a bit of the folklore surrounding each plant. I've read what biographies I could find of Linnaeus, the merry-hearted eighteenth-century Swedish genius who selected the Latin names for most of the flowers. His enjoyment of Latin and Greek mythology and his lively sense of humor are evident in the meanings behind many of the names, even after several centuries.

I became a regular visitor to the library. I bought as many books as I could afford. Friends became aware of my fascination with the subject and gave me more books on the subject. These books and the notebook that I keep have been a part of my life for over 15 years.

My collection of watercolors and the information I've compiled over the years about my wildflowers has given me a deeper appreciation of their importance and place in our lives. I've discovered that a study of wildflowers is also a study of botany, history, and geography. There were times when the economy of Europe rose and fell with the supply of, and demand for, flower bulbs. In the age of exploration, every ship carried a respected botanist whose job it was to locate and bring back to the Old World new plants selected not only for their food and medicinal value but also for their beauty. There is a story of a female botanist disguised as a man who was successful in discovering new plants in the Canary Islands until observant natives kidnapped her!

There are many legends about flowers, some probably true. The king of the Franks, entrapped by the Goths on a riverbank, is supposed to have seen iris growing throughout the river bed. He realized then that the water must be fairly shallow in places, so he and his army walked across the river and escaped. In gratitude, when Charles V became king of France, he chose the iris, or fleur-de-lis, for the royal emblem of France.

Another interesting tale I have found reveals that Josephine, wife of Napoleon, was intensely jealous of Marie Antoinette and so determined to have a more beautiful flower garden that she hired English botanists to tend her garden because she believed them to be more skillful than French botanists available at the time. They came to France in the midst of the war between France and England, because, of course, gardening transcended war. It is further written that English naval captains were instructed to deliver to France, by some means, any plants found on a captured French ship that were destined for Josephine. It was in her legendary garden that camellias imported from Asia were first grown in Europe, and it was there that the wild rose was developed into the hybrid tea rose we know today.

The early settlers of this country found a wealth of native flora which provided not only beauty, but, with some guidance from friendly Indians, food, medicine, and dyes for homespun materials. But the settlers also brought plants from home with them, which were almost as important to them as their clothes and household possessions.

Physicians brought plants used in their practice of medicine; farmers brought grain and produce seeds to sustain their new life; and the women surely tucked their favorite flower seeds into the baggage to remind them of the home they were leaving.

But many of our wildflowers also entered the New World by accident: flower seeds could have been caught in the dried plant fibers that were used as packing materials; seeds could have been imbedded in the mud of animal's hooves or caught in their fur. Even those flowers planted so lovingly in the colonies' first flower gardens may eventually have escaped the garden walls and become part of our native landscape.

I've learned that although our cultural ties are with Europe, our true botanical ties are with Asia. Many species of our native wildflowers are also natives of the Far East, lending support to the theory that the North American and Asian continents were joined at one time in the development of the earth.

The watercolors in this book were *not* done for publication; they are merely pages out of my notebook. The wildflowers I selected to share from my collection were chosen simply on the basis that they are my favorites, and I love them. They represent but an infinitesimal sampling of the myriad of spe-

cies found in the eastern United States. I hope your favorites are among these, too.

Botanists sometimes differ about the names of plants and their particular spellings, both common and botanical. To compound the confusion, many wildflowers have several common names. The names used in this book are the ones I am most familiar with, but I have tried to mention other popular names whenever possible.

Along with the watercolors, I have attempted to give you some of the interesting folklore behind each flower and some very basic descriptive information in hopes that you will be inspired to try to identify the wildflowers in your area. But this is *not* intended as a reference book, and I must emphasize that the notes about a plant's medicinal properties *must not* be taken seriously. Although sometimes chemically logical, a plant's medicinal value was most often very overrated in the early years of our country's development, and I often wonder if the plant was actually anything more than a placebo.

I offer the descriptions and folklore because I feel the people who put their love of nature into a needlework project might want to know a little about the flowers they are ''stitching up.'' The charts were designed with every effort made to be as accurate as possible as to size, shape, and color.

My passion for wildflowers has naturally led me to be concerned over the real danger that some of our plants may become extinct. Please don't destroy nature's wild beauty to develop a garden of your own. Write, instead, to one of the following major suppliers of wildflower bulbs and seeds: Geo. W. Park Seed Company, Inc., P. O. Box 31, Greenwood, South Carolina 29646; Herbst Bros. Seedsmen, Inc., 1000 N. Main Street, Brewster, New York 10509; Carroll Abbott's Green Horizons, 400 Thompson Drive, Kerrville, Texas 78029.

However, if you insist on adding wildflowers that you find in the wild to your existing garden, first make sure the soil and light conditions are suitable for the wildflowers to survive. Then, don't dig up more than one-third of the same species of plant growing in any one place unless the area is to be cleared for construction. Watch for advertised wildflower digs in your area where new construction is planned.

Whether you commune with Mother Nature at a fast clip on a bicycle, at medium speeds jogging or walking, or at a snail's pace as I do—crawling through the woods and fields—you cannot help being overcome by her exquisite detail. Wildflowers are precious gifts Nature awards her guests.

Silky Camellia
Stewartia malacodendron
Tea family

Mountain Camellia
Stewartia ovata
Tea family

These two species of wild camellias are not as prolific as most other wildflowers, making their discovery a rare treat. There are numerous types of *Stewartia* in cultivation. The botanical name honors England's John Stuart, Earl of Bute. *Stewartia* was originally spelled as you see it here, but a few purists have attempted to amend the spelling to match the name—*Stuartia*. Some manuals adhere to this amended version, but the most widely accepted spelling is the former.

Both species of *Stewartia* shown here are natives of the southeastern United States; the remaining species are native to Asia. The Silky Camellia (left), also called the Virginian Stewartia, grows in moist woods and along stream banks of the coastal plain from Virginia to Florida and west to Arkansas and Louisiana.

The Mountain Camellia (right), or Mountain Stewartia as it is often called, also prefers rich woods and stream banks. But this species is hardy at higher elevations than its lowland relative. It may be found in the Blue Ridge and Appalachian Plateau south to Alabama and Georgia. It is also hardy as far north as Pennsylvania and costal Massachusetts.

These two species are very similar, but subtle differences aid in distinguishing between the camellias. Both are tall, graceful shrubs or small trees. The Silky Camellia rarely exceeds 15 feet high, while the Mountain Camellia usually grows just a little taller.

The spectacular, creamy white blossoms of the Silky and Mountain Camellia are 2½ to 3½ inches in diameter. Each cup-shaped flower has five scalloped-edged petals and a central tuft of yellow surrounded by purplish filaments. In their native habitat, the blossoms of the Silky Camellia are the first *Stewartia* to appear (May to June), whereas the Mountain Camellia is one of the latest species to bloom (June to July).

Both species have oval-shaped leaves that are glossy and bronze tinted. Silky Camellia leaves are 1½ to 3 inches long; Mountain Camellia's run 2 to 6 inches long and have very sharp points. The leaves of both species display an unusual quilted effect due to their deeply impressed veins. Their foliage turns a rich orange, golden yellow, or bronzy wine in the autumn.

Stewartias are relatively rare in the wild state and are coveted as cultivated plants by knowledgeable gardeners. Perhaps your best opportunity to see these prizes is in a botanical garden.

(Chart appears on page 70.)

Carolina Pink
Silene caroliniana
Pink family

Members of the Pink family are often identified by their square stems, although the Mint family is also known to have square stems. Run your fingers down the stem of a plant you are having trouble identifying; if the stem is four-sided rather than cylindrical, the plant may be one of the pinks. The stems of the Carolina Pink are sticky, and usually grow no taller than 8 inches.

The dainty, five-petaled blossoms are 1 inch in diameter and can vary in color from palest pink to near scarlet. Grayish hairs are present on both sides of the tapering leaves, which are 2 to 4 inches long.

Carolina Pink bears a resemblance to phlox. Search for the shade-loving plants from New Hampshire to South Carolina and Alabama in the spring. Look among rocks where the soil is rich and well drained.

(Chart appears on page 68.)

Lupine
Lupinus perennis
Pea family

"Wolf," from the Latin *lupus*, is hardly a fitting name for so gorgeous a wildflower. The name alludes to the ancient notion that these beautiful plants robbed the soil of nutrients. Facts have proven that just the opposite is true: members of this genus have nitrogen-fixing bacteria in their root nodules.

Despite the misleading common and botanical names, Lupine is favored for its erect spires (1 to 2 feet high) of clear blue flowers from April to July and for its bright green, wheel-shaped leaves. Perhaps the most famous of all Lupines is the Texas Bluebonnet.

Although most Lupines are native to the western half of the United States, this particular variety is found in sandy soil and dry clearings from the Great Lakes east and down the eastern coast of the United States. The plant's long, woody tap root penetrates deep into dry sandy earth in search of water.

Indians are said to have used the Lupine to help in childbirth and for treating sterility.

(Chart appears on page 67.)

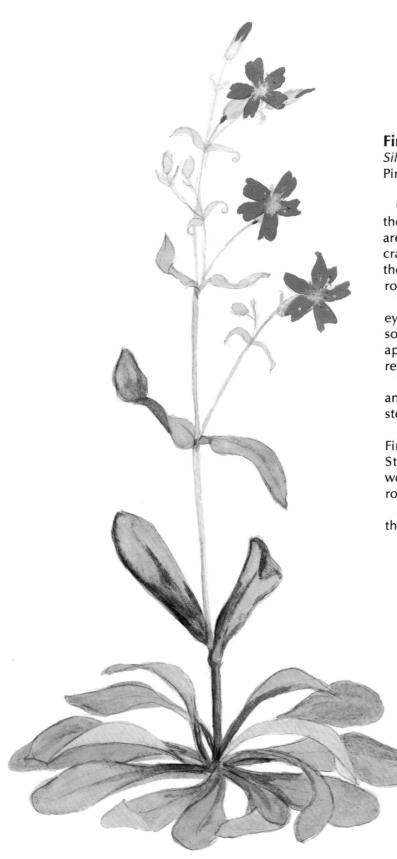

Fire Pink
Silene virginica
Pink family

Catchfly is another name for many members of the Pink family because their stems and tubular parts are coated with a sticky secretion that traps flies and crawling insects, preventing them from collecting the flowers' nectar. The Fire Pink is not a carnivorous plant.

The star-shaped blossoms of the Fire Pink are eye-catchers with five, notched petals of fiery crimson. Each flower is about 1 inch in diameter and appears along a slender hairy stem that usually reaches a height of 1 to 2 feet.

The oval, dark green leaves are 2 to 5 inches long and wider at the tip than where they join to the stem.

April to September are blooming months for the Fire Pink in the southeastern and central United States. Look for their bright blossoms in open woods, along rocky slopes, and in dry areas along roadsides.

At one time, herb doctors used a tonic made from the Fire Pink as a worm medicine.

(Chart appears on page 66.)

Indian Strawberry
Duchesnea indica
Rose family

This wonderful creeping plant can cover bare spots in your lawn with a green mat that is freckled with yellow blossoms and red fruit in the spring. Indian Strawberry thrives in poor soil in lawns and waste places, but, like all wildflowers, it will not survive where foot traffic is heavy.

Mock Strawberry and Snakeberry are other common names for this species which has become naturalized in North America. This genus differs from what most people regard as wild strawberries in that the fruit of the Indian version is smaller and not as tasty as its wild cousin. Indian Strawberry flowers are also smaller and the plant grows more rapidly than its relative.

The leaflets of the Indian Strawberry are grouped in threes, each with serrated edges. The delicate yellow flowers measure ½ inch in diameter and have five petals each.

The bright red fruit resembles the cultivated strawberry in basic shape and coloring, and it is edible but tasteless. Unlike most plants, the fruit and the flowers appear at the same time—a lovely combination of color and texture.

(Chart appears on page 63.)

Wild Azalea
Rhododendron sp.
Heath family

Clouds of springtime colors beckon visitors to the Appalachian and southern woods each year as the different species of wild azalea burst into bloom. Truly these wildflowers are unparalleled for sheer beauty.

There are approximately 18 different species of wild azaleas, and although most are concentrated in the upland woods of Appalachia, there are some species that extend farther south, as well as one West Coast native. Identification of the different species is often difficult because many have hybridized profusely in cultivation and in nature.

Colors and shades of wild azaleas range anywhere from snow white to a crimson red. Intermediate shades include yellows, oranges, corals, and salmons, and innumerable combinations of these hues.

Sizes and shapes of the different species vary as greatly as their colors. One of the South's most beautiful wild azaleas is called Pink Shell Azalea *(R. vaseyi).* A graceful, spreading shrub that grows up to 15 feet high, it is covered with clear pink blossoms in late April or early May. This species is equally gorgeous in the fall when its clear green foliage turns bright yellow orange before dropping its leaves.

Flame Azalea *(R. calendulaceum)* is another beauty that is fairly easy to distinguish from other species because of its downy leaves and striking color: pale yellow to flaming orange. Flame Azaleas are shrub-shaped and grow 5 to 10 feet high in dry open forests of oak and pine.

The Dutch, who settled thickly in the middle states, named a wild pink-blooming azalea Pinxter-flower *(R. periclymenoides).* "Pinxter" is the Dutch dialect word for "Whitsunday," which is the time this species usually begins blooming. Its faintly fragrant flowers open before the apple-green leaves appear.

This species is often called Wild Honeysuckle and Swamp Honeysuckle because of the long-tubed, trumpet-shaped flowers. Pinxter-flower stalks are covered with tiny stiff hairs, and the flower petals are hairy on the outside.

Although there are many other types equally as spectacular as the three mentioned, these are among the most popular. In any color or size, wild azaleas are an undisputed favorite among wildflower lovers.

(Chart appears on page 64.)

Yellow Jessamine
Gelsemium sempervirens
Logania family

Masses of trumpet-shaped clear yellow flowers and a delicious perfume make finding this dainty vine a special delight.

The twining evergreen vine with slender brown stems sometimes climbs to a height of 20 feet or more but does not strangle trees. The Yellow Jessamine's native habitat is woodlands and thickets, but it has been known to grow in open land especially along sunny fence rows.

Not really a jasmine, although it is often called that, Yellow Jessamine is the state flower of South Carolina and is often called Carolina Jessamine. It blooms from March to early May, with flowers grouped in small clusters or arranged singly on the vine.

All parts of the Yellow Jessamine are poisonous if eaten, but not to the touch. At one time, a medicine was concocted from the plant and used to treat mental disorders, but this practice was discontinued because of the severity of the reactions that it caused; sometimes it proved fatal. Because it is poisonous, be sure to keep children and pets away from this beauty.

(Chart appears on page 60.)

Wild Man of the Earth
Ipomoea pandurata
Morning-glory family

The most striking characteristic about this true morning glory is its enormous fleshy root that can extend as long as 12 feet and weigh 15 to 20 pounds! The root contains a milky juice and was roasted by North American Indians for food in times of famine. Because of the edible root, this species is often called Wild Potato Vine.

Ipomoea, the botanical name, comes from the Greek words *ipis,* meaning "worm" and *homoios* for "resembling," so named because of the plant's twining habit. Wild Man of the Earth is considered a trailing plant, climbing only when it is shaded, and then weakly. It makes a striking groundcover on sunny, sandy banks, and its favored habitat is in dry thickets and woods from Connecticut to Florida and west to Texas.

The bright green leaves are shaped like hearts and are 2 to 6 inches long. The handsome, trumpet-shaped blossoms are white, 3 inches in diameter, with a lavender or crimson throat.

This species is fairly easy to identify during the blooming months of May to September.

(Chart appears on page 58.)

Bring the freshness and colors of nature indoors with pillows made from your favorite wildflowers. The large blossoms of Wild Man of the Earth and the delicately twining Yellow Jessamine designs cross stitched against a background of sky blue are irresistible additions to solarium, living room, or boudoir.

Prickly Pear Cactus
Opuntia sp.
Cactus family

Beautiful and dangerous are the incongruent adjectives that best describe the Prickly Pear Cactus.

Its beauty lies in the large fragile-looking flowers that appear in May and June. The bright yellow blossoms open to 2 to 3 inches in diameter. The plant's unusual fruit is pear shaped, 1 to 1½ inches long, reddish, and edible. Oddly enough, the fruit is called Tuna.

The leaves of the Prickly Pear Cactus are not the thick green joints you see surrounding the flower; these are the stems. The leaves are actually minute, inconspicuous scales that appear briefly and then fall off.

The plant's danger is in the flat, green, jointed stems you see that are shaped like a beaver tail. Each joint is studded with tiny, wickedly barbed prickles that can cause a great deal of pain to the skin. These nearly ineradicable prickles can also work into the flesh, causing an irritating rash.

The Prickly Pear Cactus, also called Indian Fig, is the hardiest cactus in the East. A native of eastern United States, this cactus grows in rocks and sandy soil and thrives by the sea. Under proper conditions it can spread into a veritable groundcover. Look for its blossoms (but beware of the prickles!) from Minnesota south to Oklahoma and east to the coast.

Indians were said to have used the peeled stems of the Prickly Pear Cactus as a bandage to bind wounds. On the other hand, explorers probably viewed the plant as a nuisance and one to be avoided, except perhaps in the spring when its sunny blossoms appeared to grace the prairies.

(Chart appears on page 56.)

Purple Joe-Pye Weed
Eupatorium purpureum
Composite family

Joe Pye was an Indian herb doctor in colonial New England who reportedly used one species of this plant to stop a typhus epidemic in Massachusetts. The common name honors his efforts. The botanical name honors Eupator, a biblical herb doctor.

Joe-Pye Weed is not a weed at all, but is actually an herb. The plant was used by colonists to treat gout, rheumatism, dropsy, kidney stones, and diarrhea by boiling its roots to make a tonic. They also used the tonic as a stimulant. Woodsmen used the stems of Hollow Joe-Pye Weed *(E. fistulosum)* as a drinking straw.

Indian women believed a bath made from boiling the roots of the Joe-Pye Weed would strengthen a baby. If the bath did not produce immediate results, the child was often subjected to Joe-Pye Weed baths until he was six years old.

Huge, fuzzy, flat-topped blossoms make the beautiful Purple Joe-Pye Weed easy to spot from July to September in thickets, along stream banks, and in low, open woods. It can be found as far west as Oklahoma. Although it usually grows 2 to 6 feet high, it can reach a height of 12 feet in some of the low, moist areas of the South.

Flowers range in color from creamy white to pale pink to lavender. The blossom heads are rounded, or somewhat pyramidal in shape. The long, serrate leaves grow in groups along the stem. The purple or black markings at the leaf joints help distinguish the Purple Joe-Pye Weed from other species of Joe-Pye Weeds.

Another identifying trait is the vanilla odor emitted when the plant is crushed or bruised.

Names that might be more familiar to some for the Purple Joe-Pye Weed are Queen-of-the-Meadow, Trumpetweed, Feverweed, and Kidney-root.

(Chart appears on page 62.)

Tickseed Coreopsis
Coreopsis lanceolata
Composite family

"Miniature sunflowers" is an apt description of these bright blossoms that are borne on long, slender stems. Each yellow flower head is 1 to 2 inches in diameter and has six to ten (but usually eight) notched petals. The center of each flower is yellow to reddish brown. As the blossom fades, the center turns brown and produces tiny seeds that look much like ticks. This accounts for its common name, Tickseed Coreopsis, and for its botanical name: from the Greek *coris*, meaning "a bug" and *opis*, meaning "appearance."

Their large showy flowers make many coreopsis favorite cultivated plants. Most types will bloom all summer if you keep the flowers picked, but if left unpicked, will reseed themselves to provide plenty of new plants each year. In nature, the Tickseed Coreopsis blooms from May to August in dry, sandy or rocky woods, clearings, or thickets, and along roadsides.

Our forefathers boiled the stems of the Atlantic or Tall Coreopsis *(C. tripteris)* and used the tonic as a remedy for internal pains, particularly when they were unsure of the origin of the pain and there were signs of internal bleeding.

Other species of this wildflower are identified by their different leaf shapes. While the Tickseed Coreopsis has lance-shaped leaves (much longer than wide), the leaves of the Atlantic Coreopsis are palmatic, (resembling outspread fingers), and the Whorled Tickseed *(C. verticillata)* has deeply segmented leaves attached in circles around the stems.

(Chart appears on page 55.)

Red Clover
Trifolium pratense
Pea family

Masses of grape-scented Red Clover seen growing along highways are a familiar pleasure to travelers from May to August. Besides the beauty of the dense, rounded heads and chevron-marked leaves, Red Clover is a valuable cultivated plant because it acts as a soil builder, adding organic matter and improving the nitrogen content of the soil.

In areas where road construction has destroyed the topsoil, clover is often planted to help prevent further erosion and to enrich the existing soil. This tall (8 to 18 inches high) wildflower is also planted with hay in dairy country to improve soil nutrients.

The fact that it is a valuable nectar source for bees accounts for the widespread distribution of Red Clover. It is found throughout North America.

The distinctive three-lobed clover leaf is believed by many to be the original shamrock. The name "clover" is a corruption of the latin word *clava*, meaning "club," so named because of the leaf's resemblance to the club carried by Hercules. This explains why a clover leaf is called a club on playing cards.

Red Clover was a popular plant with the pioneers for its medicinal value. Tea made from the dried flower heads was used as a remedy for boils and similar skin problems, while coughs and hoarseness were treated with a mixture of the tea plus onions and honey. Indians used the clover leaves in salads, soups, and stews.

(Chart appears on page 54.)

Queen Anne's Lace
Daucus carota
Carrot family

Who among us would not recognize the lacy white umbrellas and delicate feathery leaves of Queen Anne's Lace? The large flower heads (4 to 8 inches in diameter) are actually made up of clusters of tiny white flowers, each with an almost indiscernible center of purple. Its most popular common name originated from the plant's resemblance to the stiff white collars of lace worn by Queen Anne of England.

Wild Carrot is another common name for this favorite wildflower, since it is a close relative of the common garden carrot. The fleshy root resembles a carrot, and the leaves give off a carrot odor when crushed. When cooked, the roots can be eaten, but excessive quantities will turn one's skin yellow.

Indians used the plant to treat liver diseases; seeds were used to treat coughs, dysentery and colic and also as seasoning for stews and soups.

This stately European immigrant grows 1 to 5 feet high throughout the summer in dry fields and waste places from Quebec to Florida.

The exquisite flowers are a wonderful addition to any cut arrangement and may be dried effectively.

(Chart appears on page 52.)

Sundrops

Oenothera fruticosa
Evening-primrose family

Most members of the Evening-primrose family open their blossoms in the evening, as the name suggests, and wilt the following morning. But Sundrops, true to its common name, prefers to display its large (1 to 2 inches in diameter), bright yellow blossoms in the sunshine.

This day-blooming species stands 1 to 3 feet high and has narrow, oblong leaves. Look for Sundrops' showy blossoms between April and August along roadsides and open places in dry, sandy soil as far west as Oklahoma.

Indians used to eat the seed pods of Sundrops. The young, tender stems and leaves are still eaten as cooked greens, and its boiled roots taste much like parsnip.

(Chart appears on page 51.)

Blue-eyed Grass

Sisyrinchium graminoides
Iris family

Sunny mornings from April to July are the best time to search for these tiny, violet-blue flowers with yellow centers. The scentless blossoms last only one day and close in the afternoon or immediately upon being picked.

Look for this petite member of the Iris family in meadows, woods edges and grasslands. It thrives in a partly shaded wildflower or rock garden and will produce abundant seedlings.

Blue-eyed Mary or Star-eyed Grass, as this species is sometimes called, is actually not a grass at all, but its narrow, grasslike leaves and slightly flattened stems account for the common names.

Blue-eyed Grass grows from 6 to 24 inches high with flowers ½ inch in diameter. Many types of Blue-eyed Grass are yellow, white, or purple, making identification of this species relatively difficult. Most are found in the eastern half of the United States and adjacent Canada.

(Chart appears on page 50.)

Dwarf Crested Iris
Iris cristata
Iris family

Iris, Greek for "rainbow," is a fitting name when the different species come in so many beautiful colors: red, yellow, blue, violet, and white. The Dwarf Crested Iris ranges in shades of blue/purple, from pale lilac to a gorgeous deep violet. A downy yellow blotch appears at the base of each petal.

This tiny beauty (4 to 9 inches high) is aptly termed "dwarf" because its blossoms are usually shorter than its slender bright green leaves. The flower appears rather over-sized (2 to 3 inches in diameter) for so short a plant. It blooms in April and May.

There are approximately 100 species of iris growing in the rich woodlands of the southeastern states. The iris grows from a rhizome, which was cultivated by the Indians and used extensively as a cathartic and, in pulverized form, as a poultice for bruises and sores.

(Chart appears on page 47.)

Passion Flower
Passiflora incarnata
Passion flower family

Early Spanish explorers reportedly used the distinctive Passion Flower to illustrate Christianity to the Indians. The fringe represented either a halo or the crown of thorns; the five stamens, the wounds of Christ; the five sepals and five petals, the 10 faithful disciples ; and the three-knobbed stigmas , three nails used to nail Him to the cross.

Whether the Indians understood these elements of the crucifixion or not, they recognized some medicinal value in the Passion Flower. By pulverizing the plant's roots, Indians and colonists alike concocted a potion that supposedly relieved insominia and acted as a sedative.

The Passion Flower is a twining vine that can reach lengths of 10 to 20 feet. The fragrant blossoms range in color from white to lavender and are 2 to 3 inches in diameter.

The large, showy flowers are not the only distinctive feature of this plant. The fragrant yellow fruit grows to the size and shape of a lemon and is edible when ripe; hence the common name Wild Apricot. Maypop, another common name, comes from the popping sound made by the fruit when it is opened.

Watch for the Passion Flower in thickets and fields from Virginia to Florida and west to Texas. It blooms from May to August.

(Chart appears on page 48.)

Rich moist soil and filtered sun make summer forests favorite hiding places for native wildflowers. Flowering Dogwood clouds the woods with white blossoms and are cross stitched here to grace a wall in your home. Blossoms of the Dwarf Crested Iris enliven the top of a small box. And Tickseed Coreopsis, Orange Milkwort, and Sundrops designs cross stitched and set beneath a shield of glass make a stunning tray for warm weather entertaining.

Purple Trillium
Trillium erectum
Lily family

Trillium means "three," and the flowers suit their name with three petals, three sepals, and three leaves. Even its berry has either three or six sides.

The flowers (about 2 inches in diameter) are borne on 12-inch-high stems, a single flower on each stem. The petals curve back toward the stem. Because of its drooping head, Purple Trillium is often overlooked in the cool shade of rich woods where it grows. The best time to search for this unusual wildflower is from March to June from Quebec to the Georgia mountains and west to Tennessee.

Other common names for the Purple Trillium include Stinking Willie, Stinking Benjamin, or Wet-Dog Trillium because of the extremely foul odor emitted from this dark-colored wildflower. In fairness to this beautiful flower, however, it must be added that the unpleasant odor is not strong unless you happen to be crawling around on the forest floor. One hypothesis is that the Purple Trillium, like many plants, only releases its "perfume" at certain times to attract its pollinators.

Some trilliums are not as showy in color as the Purple Trillium, but are more enjoyable as cultivated plants because of their more agreeable scent. A white variety of trillium grows in the Great Smokies.

Wake-Robin is another favored name for this wildflower, so named because the maroon red flowers are blooming when the robins return to the North.

The resemblance of Purple Trillium to the color and odor of decaying flesh attracts the carrion flies responsible for pollination of the flower. Early herb doctors, who often thought that medicinal plants displayed some outward sign that revealed its particular value, used the Purple Trillium as a treatment for gangrene. Indians and early settlers chewed the plant's dried rhizomes as treatment for snakebites and diarrhea and as an anesthetic.

(Chart appears on page 46.)

Tall Goldenrod
Solidago altissima
Composite family

What child would not recognize the deep yellow plumes of goldenrod that gild roadsides and clearings? There are over 100 species of goldenrod in North America, and many look so much alike that identification is tricky. The most familiar species may be found blooming from midsummer and continue into the fall from Texas to Canada and east to the coast.

Many species share the same basic characteristics illustrated by the Tall Goldenrod. Its plume-shaped flower heads are composed of clusters of tiny yellow blossoms, arranged only on the upper side of the gently curving branches. All except one species of goldenrod are yellow to gold in color.

The lance-shaped leaves have sharply-toothed edges and decrease in size from the base of the plant to the flower head. The stem of Tall Goldenrod is smooth, pale green or purplish.

Tall Goldenrod stands up to 6 feet high, thereby aiding in its identification; most of the other species are much shorter.

Goldenrod was once valued as a remedy for intestinal disorders. A mild carminative was made from the leaves that helped relieve stomach gas.

Sinus and allergy sufferers have long blamed the prolific goldenrod for their troubles. The fact is that the pollen of the goldenrod is somewhat heavy and therefore is not easily inhaled through the nose. Ragweed, with its light, floating pollen, blooms at the same time and in the same places as goldenrod. And in most cases, it is probably the ragweed that is the culprit for hay fever sufferers, not goldenrod.

(Chart appears on page 45.)

Flowering Dogwood

Cornus florida
Dogwood family

Airy clouds of white blossoms against a background of fresh new green—Flowering Dogwood is one of our most beloved woodland sights.

There are several interesting theories as to the origin of the common name. One states that *dogwood* is a corrupted form of *dagwood,* from an Old English word for dagger, a meat skewer used by butchers. Evidently the hard wood of the tree was used to make the skewer. A second explanation of the origin is that the bark of one of the European species when boiled in water was used to wash mangy dogs. Neither theory seems very apropos for such an exquisite tree. The botanical name *Cornus* means "horn," and refers to the hardness of the wood.

Legends surrounding the dogwood are far more appropriate to the plant's beauty. In Jesus's day, the dogwood supposedly grew much taller and straighter than today's version. Christ's cross is said to have been made from the wood of this tree, which moved Jesus to promise that the dogwood would never grow so large that it could be used for this purpose again. A reminder of the dogwood's role in the Crucifixion, the petals of the dogwood flowers resemble the shape of the cross, and each tip is slightly notched and tinted brown to represent Christ's wounds.

In the filtered sun of forests, its normal habitat, the dogwood is a slender tree with an umbrella-shaped cap of spreading branches. It can grow as high as 40 feet, but is usually much shorter. In sunnier locations where it does not grow well, it becomes a bushy little tree with branches beginning close to the ground.

Dogwood flowers do not have any real petals. The large white "petals" you see are actually modified leaves that grow slowly and change from green to white as they enlarge. The true flowers are very small, greenish yellow blossoms that appear in dense clusters at the center of the four petallike leaves. Fully formed, each "blossom" measures 3 to 4 inches in diameter.

Flowering Dogwood begins blooming in March and is found in the eastern United States as far west as Kansas and Texas. The white to pink blossoms (bracts) appear before the oval-shaped leaves, and remain showy for a full month.

Autumn finds the Flowering Dogwood no less spectacular than spring. Clusters of glossy, scarlet red berries, surrounded by hues of red foliage in the fall, last until Christmas unless they are eaten by squirrels and birds. In winter, Flowering Dogwood is covered with tiny white "buttons."

Besides its obvious ornamental value, dogwood has long been used medicinally. Dogwood bark was once used to concoct a tonic for treating malaria, colic, and as a fever deterrent. A mild astringent made from dried bark was used to stop bleeding.

The wood of the dogwood is extremely heavy and hard. Because of this, it has been used to make such various articles as golf clubs, weaving shuttles, and wedges (gluts) for splitting logs. With wear, the wood becomes very smooth.

Despite its practical uses, the sheer beauty of the Flowering Dogwood is reason enough for its favored position among wildflowers.

(Chart appears on page 42.)

Sweet Bay
Magnolia virginiana
Magnolia family

The beautiful Sweet Bay grows in water accumulated in unexplained crescent-shaped depressions in the earth. These depressions, called "bays," are present along the eastern coast of the United States. Until the development of the airplane, these bays were not discernible and, although still largely unexplained, the most widely accepted belief is that they were caused by meteorites.

Though often seen as a straggling swamp plant, Sweet Bay can grow to a height of 50 feet. In fact, there is a variety in western Louisiana and eastern Texas that reaches a height of 70 feet and bears flowers 5 inches in diameter. Most of the evergreen Sweet Bay range between 12 to 25 feet high with creamy white flowers 3 inches in diameter.

The thick leathery leaves are 4 to 6 inches long, bright to dark green, with lovely silvery undersides. The leaf of this large shrub or small tree is often used as seasoning in food.

Other common names for the striking Sweet Bay are Bay Magnolia and Beaver Tree because beavers frequently use its wood. Look for the smooth, pale bark and very fragrant blossoms of the Sweet Bay in May and June in swamps and wet ground.

(Chart appears on page 40.)

Wild Ginger
Asarum canadense
Birthwort family

Named for the pungent aroma that arises when the rootstock is bruised, Wild Ginger was used by the colonists as a substitute for the tropical spice that was so hard to get in the New World. Indians also coveted the plant's roots not only for the ginger flavoring it added to foods, but for its medicinal value as well. Wild Ginger roots were used to treat whooping cough, colds, fevers, and stomach disorders. They were also cooked and used as a mild gargle and as a poultice for earaches.

The blossoms of the Wild Ginger rest directly on the ground and are of an unusual purple brown color inside with a dull brown exterior. They are cup-shaped flowers, 1 inch in diameter, with three clear divisions, but the flowers do not have any true petals. Blooming months are April to May.

The leaves of the Wild Ginger are broad heart shapes. The thick pairs of leaves are covered by very tiny hairs and usually do not extend higher than 6 inches above the ground on hairy stems.

Because of the unusual brownish coloring, Wild Ginger blossoms are often concealed by leaf litter on the forest floor. The curious must be meticulous in their search and know what to look for. Favorite habitats include rich, moist woods and hillsides of the eastern United States as far south as Alabama.

Other common names for this species include Dutchman's Pipe, Heart Leaf, and Little Brown Jug.

(Chart appears on page 44.)

Orange Milkwort
Polygala lutea
Milkwort family

Wild Bachelor's Button is another common name for this tall (6 to 20 inches high) branching plant with smooth pale green leaves and stems. The bright orange flowers are the size and shape of Red Clover and remain in bloom from June to September— quite a long time compared to most wildflowers.

Orange Milkworts grow in the southern states in sunny bogs and wet sandy flats, preferring sphagnum and other mosses indicative of strongly acid soil.

Crush the root of an Orange Milkwort plant and you'll find a wintergreen flavor; hence its other common name, Candyroot.

The botanical name *Polygala* comes from the Greek *polys,* meaning "much," and *gala,* meaning "milk." At one time, Milkworts were fed to dairy cattle and nursing mothers in the belief that the plant helped produce milk.

When dried, the bright orange blossom turns a rich golden brown. It is an ideal choice for dried arrangements since the sturdy stem retains its stiffness and does not have to be replaced.

(Chart appears on page 39.)

Dayflower
Commelina virginica
Spiderwort family

At first glance, the Dayflower appears to have only two large, rounded petals. Look more carefully and a third, lower petal becomes visible. This inequality in the three petals offers a clue to the plant's botanical name, *Commelina*. Stories are told of three Commelin brothers who lived in Holland. Two of the brothers were reknowned botanists while the third evidently displayed no interest in the subject. The two large, obvious flower petals are said to represent the brother botanists; the disinterested third brother is identified with the inconspicuous third petal.

The common name seems more logical than the botanical since the Dayflower's tiny deep blue blossoms (about ½ inch in diameter) last only one day. June to October is the best time to spot Dayflowers scattered in cool woods and along moist banks from Maine to Georgia and as far west as Minnesota and Tennessee.

Early settlers gathered the stems and leaves of the Dayflower and prepared them as one would spinach. The tender greens were also used in salads. A potion made from the blossoms was said to increase sexual potency and so was drunk by aged men and women and was even fed to stud animals.

(Chart appears on page 38.)

Violet
Viola sp.
Violet family

Familiar and unrivaled favorites, violets come in many different types, each with its own personality. Four characteristics that most violets seem to have in common are that they are low, leafy plants, rarely growing taller than 10 to 12 inches high; the flowers each have five petals; their native habitats are moist woodlands, fields, and roadsides throughout the United States; and they are loved by many wildflower enthusiasts.

Flower colors range from deep purples and blues to yellows to white, and leaf shapes vary almost as widely as the colors. Generally speaking, violets are divided into two groups: one group bears both the leaves and the flowers on the same stems; the other group has the leaves and flowers growing on separate stems from a rhizome. The following are brief descriptions of a few of the most popular and more easily identified species.

One of the most common species of purple violets with flowers and leaves on separate stalks is the Common Blue Violet *(V. papilionaceae)*. It produces flowers ¾ inch in diameter from March to June. A white variety with purple veins called Confederate Violet is found in the South. The flowers of the Common Blue Violet are known to be high in vitamin C and because of this are a nutritious addition to salads.

The pale blue Pansy Violet *(V. pedata)* boasts the largest blooms of all the violets, but its stems are short and thick. It is often called Birdsfoot or Crowfoot Violet because of the distinctive shape of the leaves. This species displays its beauty from April to June.

Large rounded leaves (2 to 4 inches in diameter) and bright yellow blossoms typify the Round-leaved Violet *(V. rotundifolia)*. This species blooms early (March to April), but its leaves are at their largest in the summer. The leaves of all yellow violets can be used to thicken stews and soups, and as a garnish in salads.

The white-flowered Canada Violet *(V. canadensis)* is the tallest member of the violet family, growing 18 to 20 inches high. Each delicate blossom has a yellowish center. Its leaves are broadly oval or heart shaped. This species blooms from late April into July and sometimes a bit later.

Look for arrow- or spade-shaped leaves, 1 to 4 inches long, pointed at the tip and squared at the base if you want to find the Arrow-leaved Violet *(V. sagittata)*. This species' blossoms are violet purple or deep blue.

Folklore is replete with tales of the medicinal and food value of violets. Indians boiled and then dried the small violet bulbs and stored them for winter food. Early settlers crushed violet seeds and leaves into poultices to treat inflamed eyes and other swellings, and pioneer children were given a mild syrup of violets and honey as a laxative. All skin and lung diseases were at one time treated with dried violet plants, and all species were reputed to have blood purifying properties.

Four states—New Jersey, Rhode Island, Illinois, and Wisconsin—have chosen the fragrant violet as their state flower.

For all their numbers and peculiarities, and despite the unending confusion in trying to identify the different species, violets are a delightful treasure for even the most casual of nature lovers.

(Charts appear on pages 34, 35, 36, and 37.)

Wildflowers bring visions of spring lushness—of feathery fern textures and ever deepening shades of green. A delicate lace-edged tablecloth is made even more lovely by a cross-stitched violet nestled diagonally in each corner. And what more dramatic way to display an exquisite piece of needlework than to inset it in a mirror frame, as with this beautifully cross-stitched Passion Flower.

Butterfly-weed
Asclepias tuberosa
Milkweed family

Masses of these brilliantly colored blossoms act as a magnet to butterflies, who are responsible for pollinating their beautiful Butterfly-weed. Although typically a glowing orange with coral undertones, Butterfly-weed flowers may range from true yellow to all shades of orange to a nearly pure red.

This spectacular landing field for butterflies is easy to spot from June to September in dry, open soil in the eastern half of the United States. It makes an excellent cut flower, but many people prefer to leave it growing in its natural habitat because it is a valuable nectar source for hummingbirds.

The 1- to 3-foot-high arching stems are covered by numerous small, hairy leaves. Unlike most members of the Milkweed family, Butterfly-weed sap is not milky but a watery juice.

Pleurisy Root is another common name for Butterfly-weed because Indians chewed the tough thick root as a cure for pleurisy and other pulmonary ailments. Indians also ate the young, tender shoots as a green vegetable, made a sugar from the flowers, and ate the boiled seed pods with their buffalo meat.

(Chart appears on page 33.)

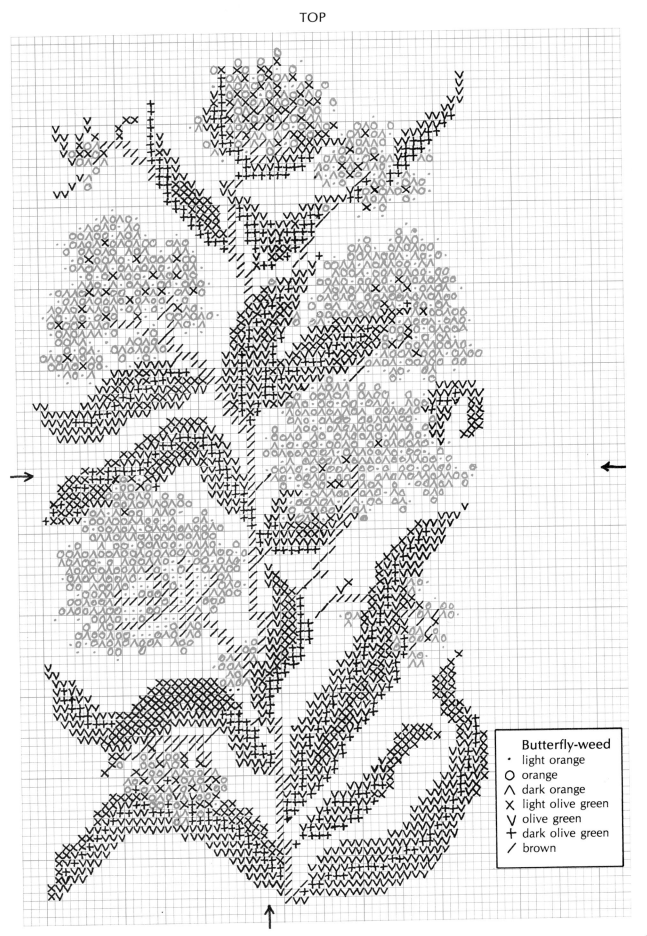

Butterfly-weed
- · light orange
- ◯ orange
- ⋀ dark orange
- ✕ light olive green
- ⋁ olive green
- ✚ dark olive green
- ╱ brown

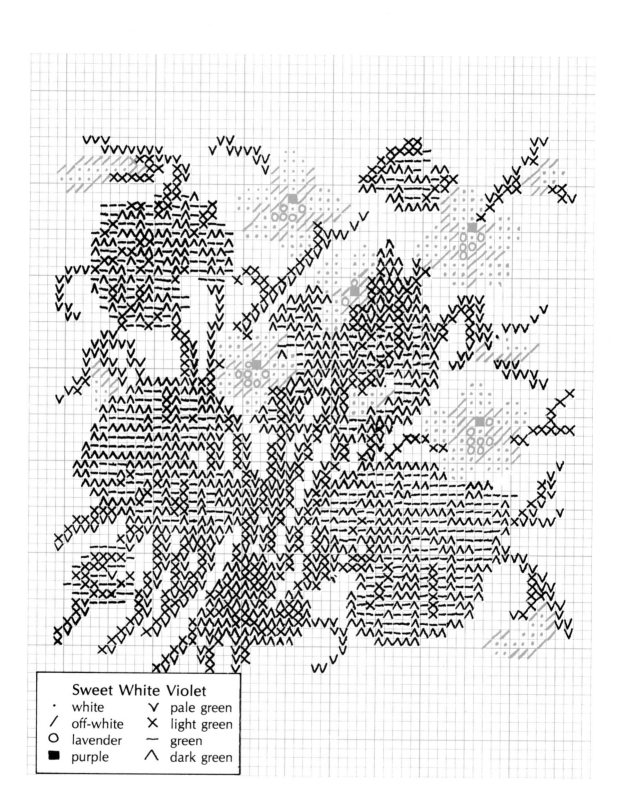

Sweet White Violet

· white	V pale green
/ off-white	X light green
O lavender	— green
■ purple	∧ dark green

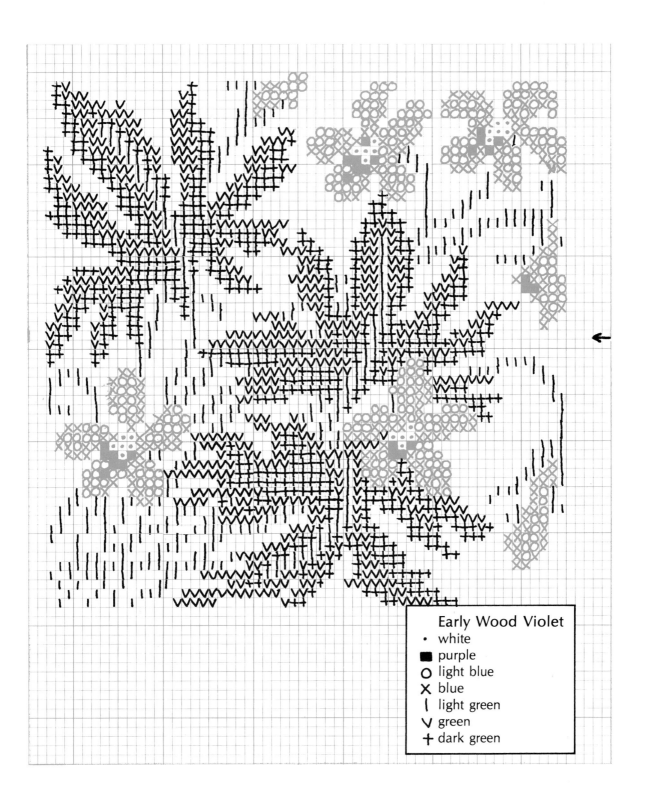

Early Wood Violet
· white
■ purple
O light blue
✗ blue
| light green
V green
+ dark green

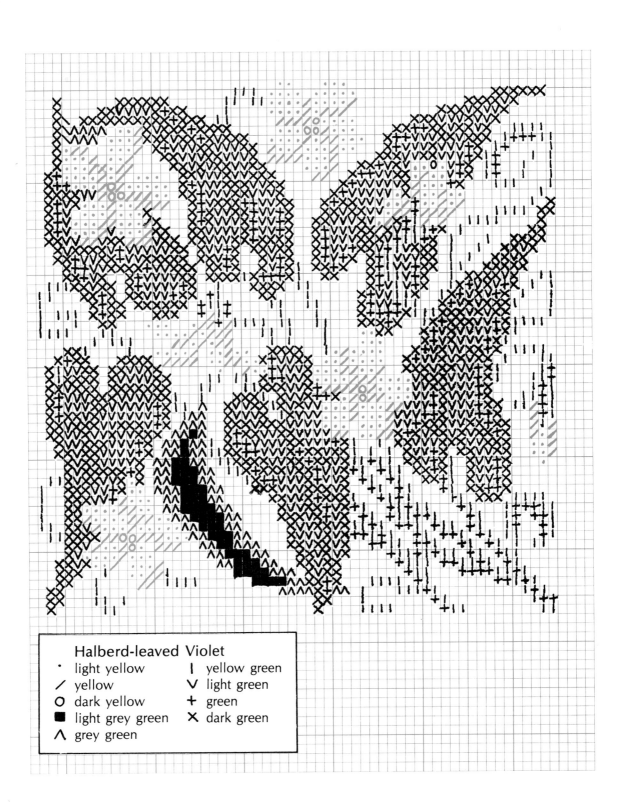

Halberd-leaved Violet

· light yellow | yellow green
/ yellow   V light green
O dark yellow   + green
■ light grey green X dark green
∧ grey green

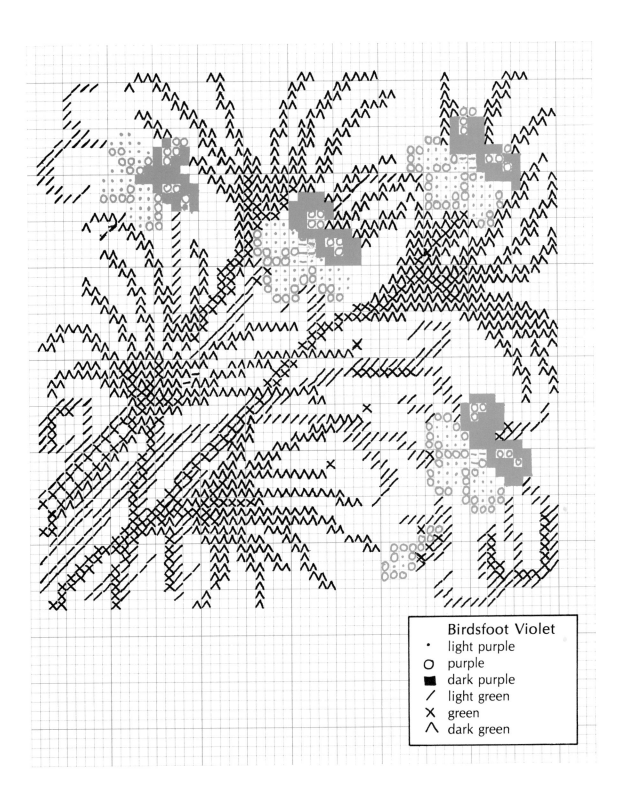

Birdsfoot Violet
- · light purple
- O purple
- ■ dark purple
- / light green
- X green
- Λ dark green

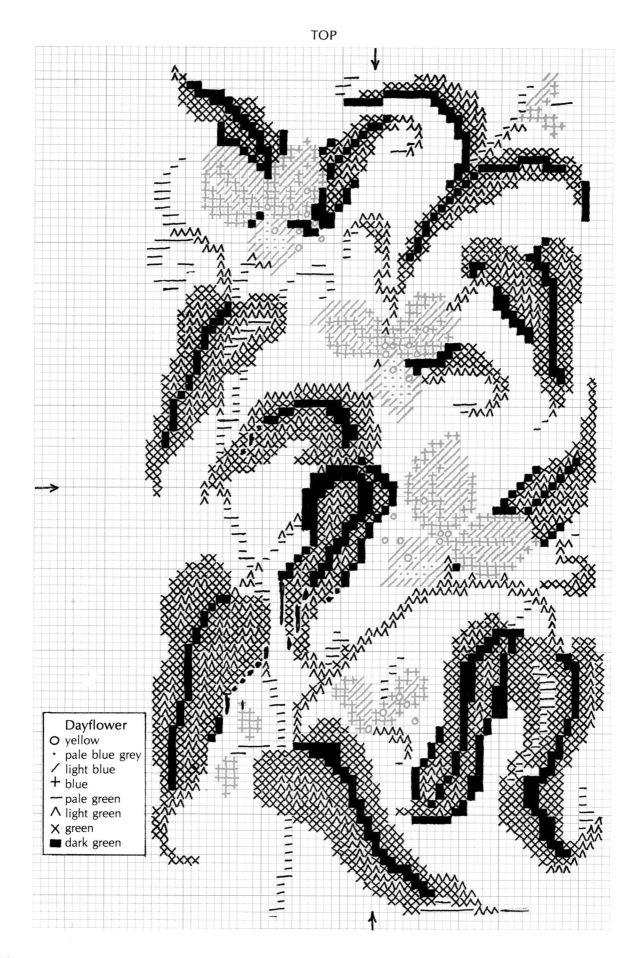

Dayflower
O yellow
• pale blue grey
/ light blue
+ blue
— pale green
∧ light green
✕ green
■ dark green

Orange Milkwort
- ■ orange
- ∧ dark orange
- • light yellow green
- / yellow green
- × olive green
- ○ dark olive green

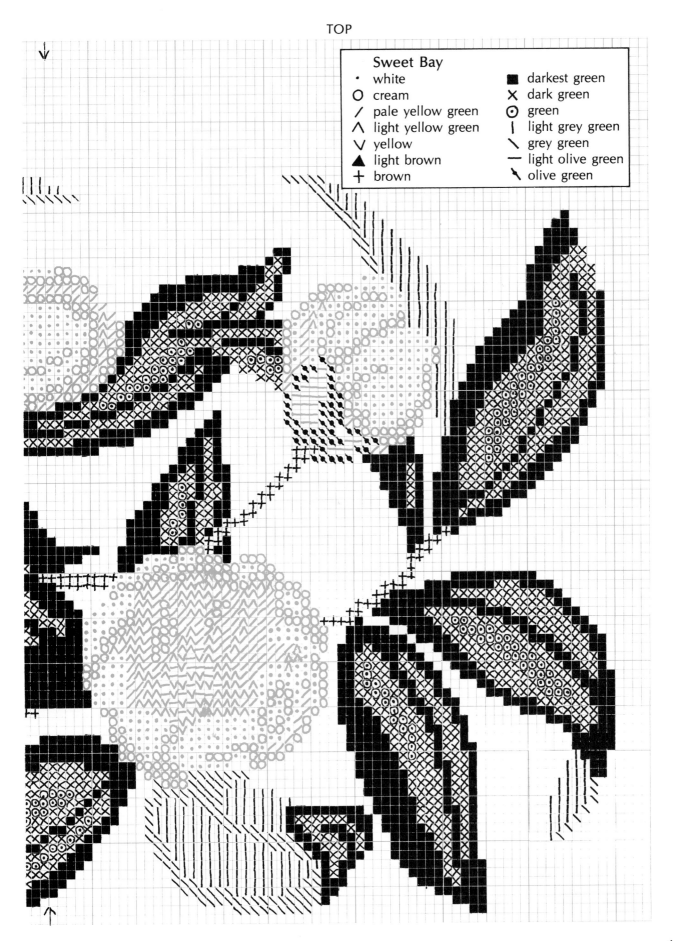

Sweet Bay
- • white
- ○ cream
- / pale yellow green
- ∧ light yellow green
- ∨ yellow
- ▲ light brown
- + brown
- ■ darkest green
- ✕ dark green
- ⊙ green
- | light grey green
- \ grey green
- — light olive green
- ＼ olive green

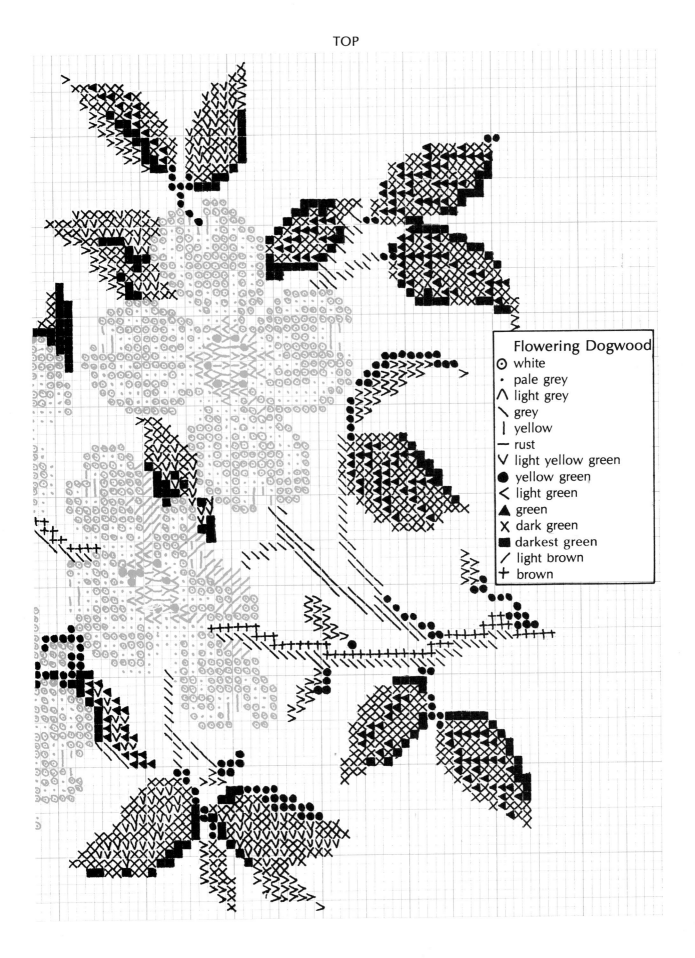

Flowering Dogwood
⊙ white
· pale grey
∧ light grey
╲ grey
│ yellow
— rust
∨ light yellow green
● yellow green
< light green
▲ green
✕ dark green
■ darkest green
╱ light brown
+ brown

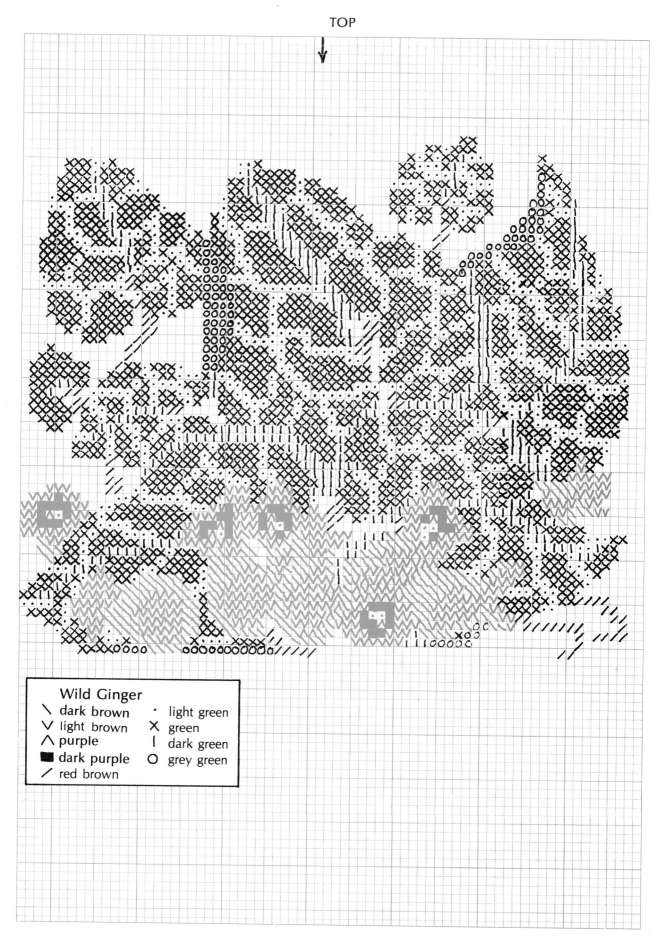

Wild Ginger
\ dark brown   · light green
V light brown   X green
∧ purple   I dark green
■ dark purple   O grey green
/ red brown

TOP

Tall Goldenrod
· yellow
\ yellow gold
X gold
/ olive green
V light green
+ green
O dark green

45

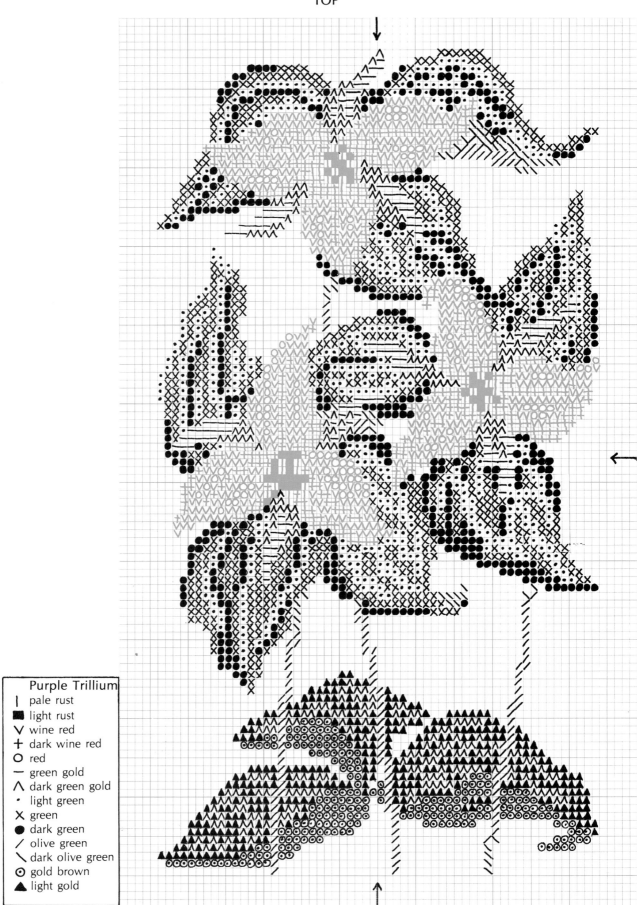

Purple Trillium
| | pale rust
■ light rust
∨ wine red
+ dark wine red
○ red
— green gold
∧ dark green gold
· light green
✕ green
● dark green
╱ olive green
╲ dark olive green
⊙ gold brown
▲ light gold

TOP
↓

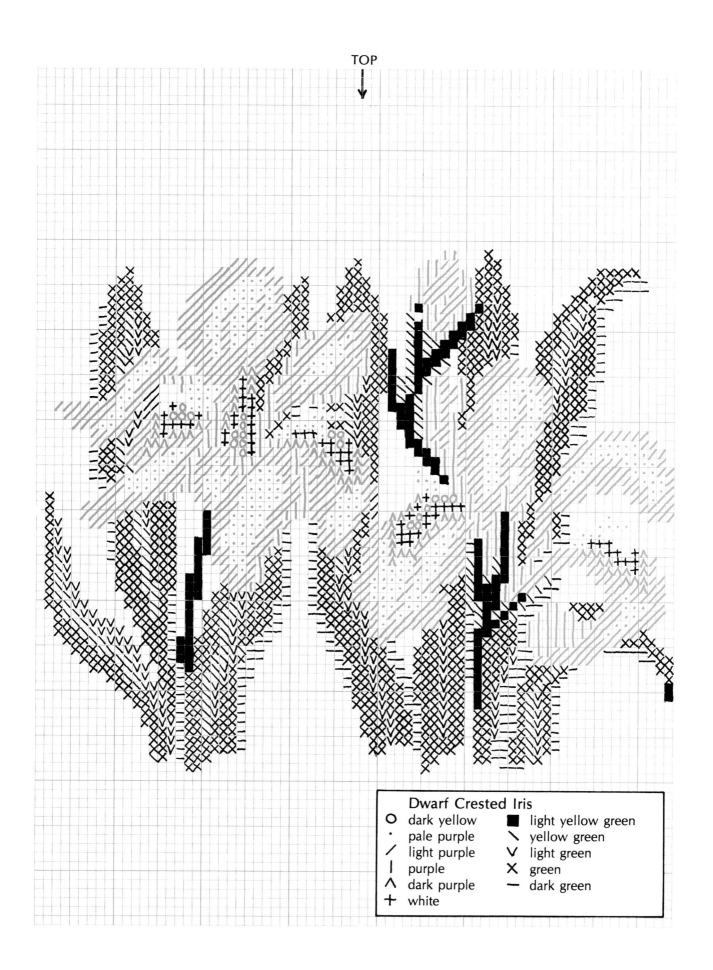

Dwarf Crested Iris

O	dark yellow	■ light yellow green
·	pale purple	\ yellow green
/	light purple	V light green
I	purple	X green
∧	dark purple	— dark green
+	white	

Passion Flower
/ light purple
O purple
■ dark purple
— peach
+ rust
\ dark rust
I light green
V green
X dark green
• light yellow
Λ yellow green
backstitching:
tendrils—
dark green

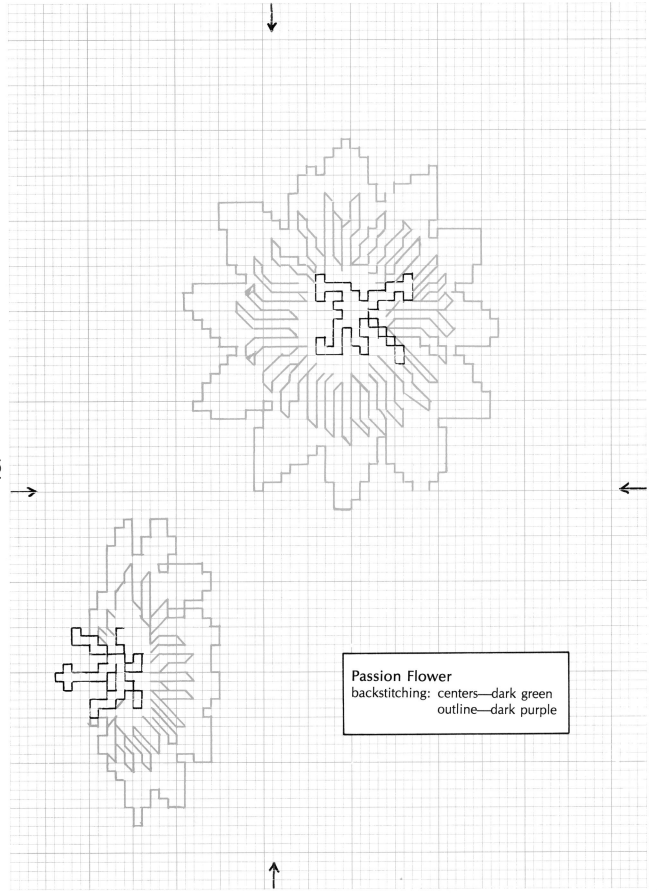

TOP

Passion Flower
backstitching: centers—dark green
            outline—dark purple

49

TOP

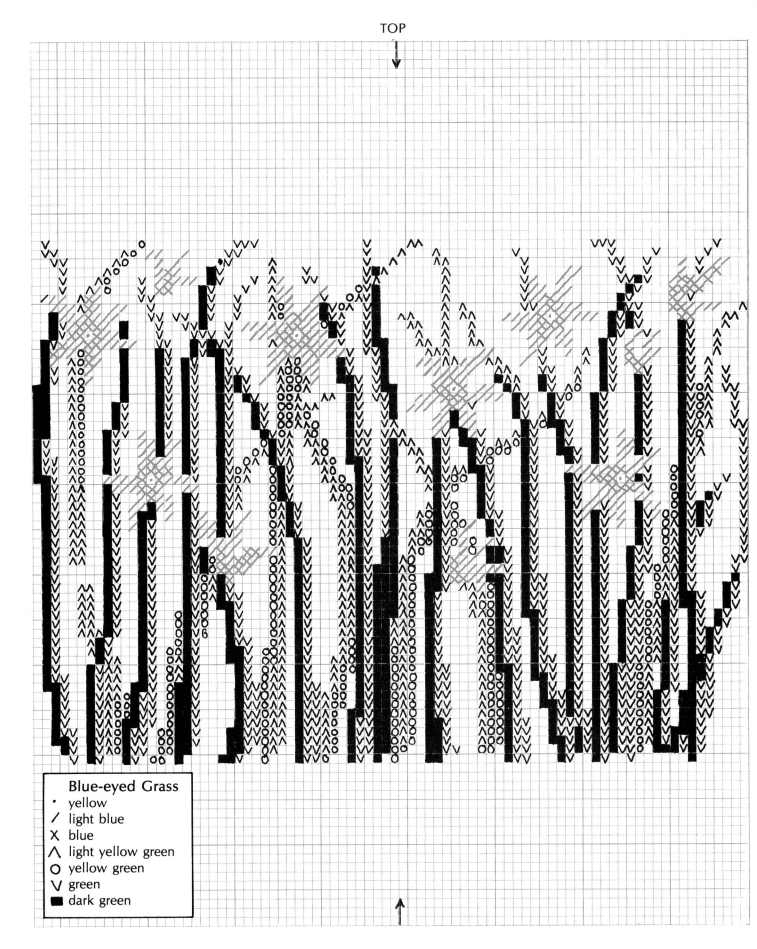

Blue-eyed Grass
- • yellow
- / light blue
- X blue
- ∧ light yellow green
- O yellow green
- V green
- ■ dark green

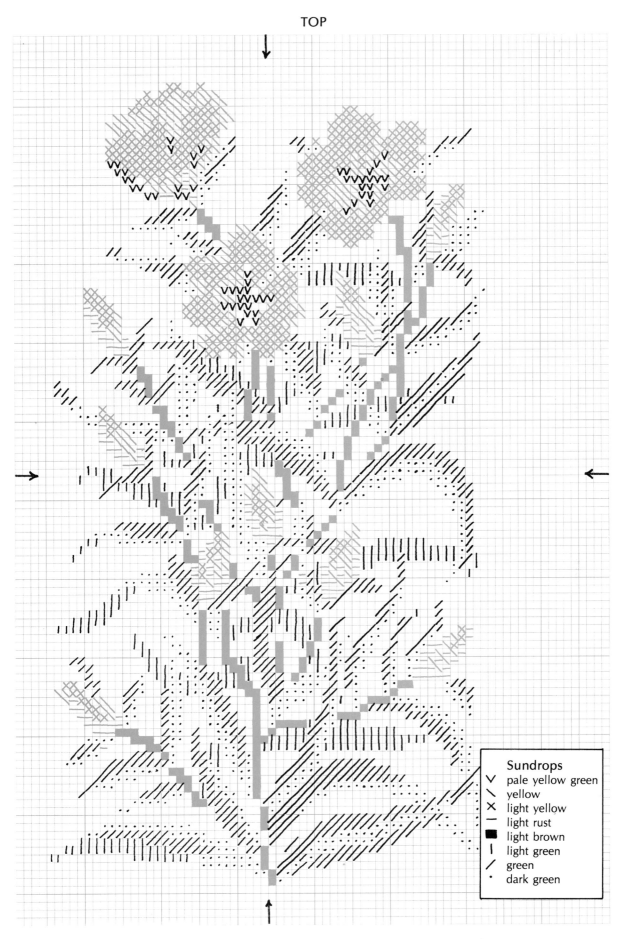

Sundrops
V pale yellow green
\ yellow
X light yellow
— light rust
■ light brown
| light green
/ green
• dark green

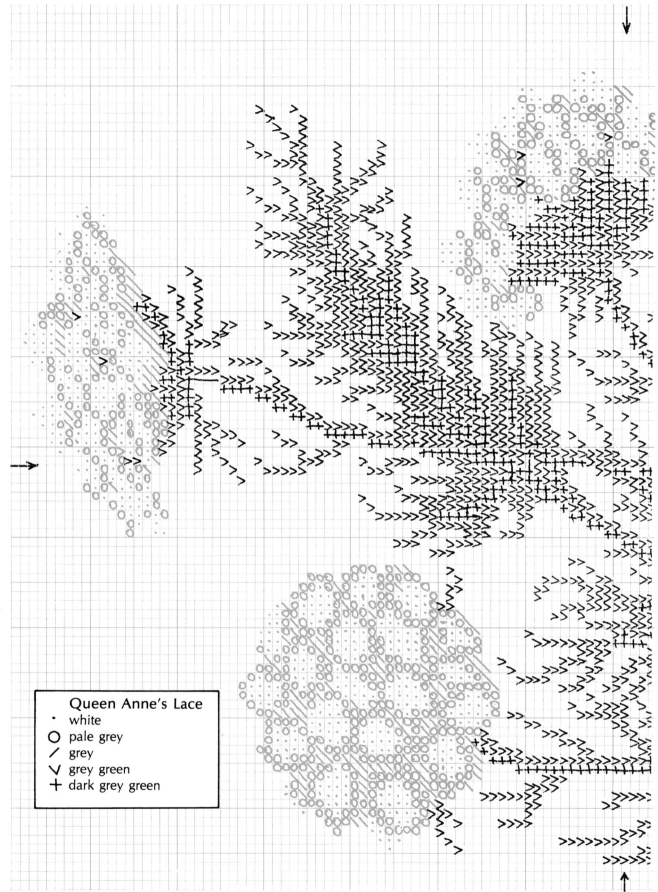

TOP

Queen Anne's Lace
- · white
- O pale grey
- / grey
- V grey green
- + dark grey green

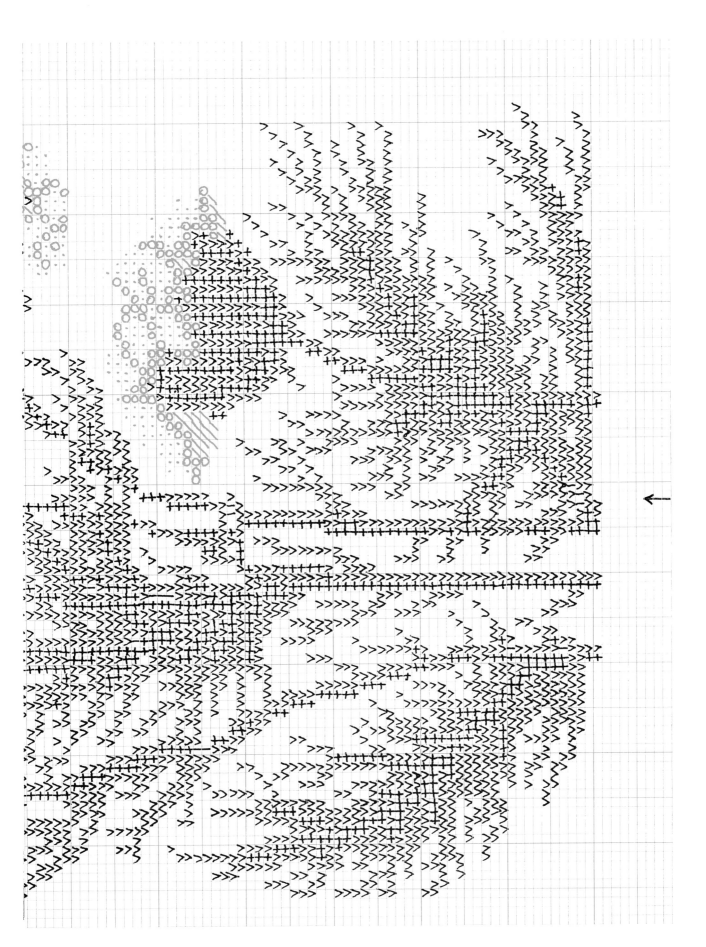

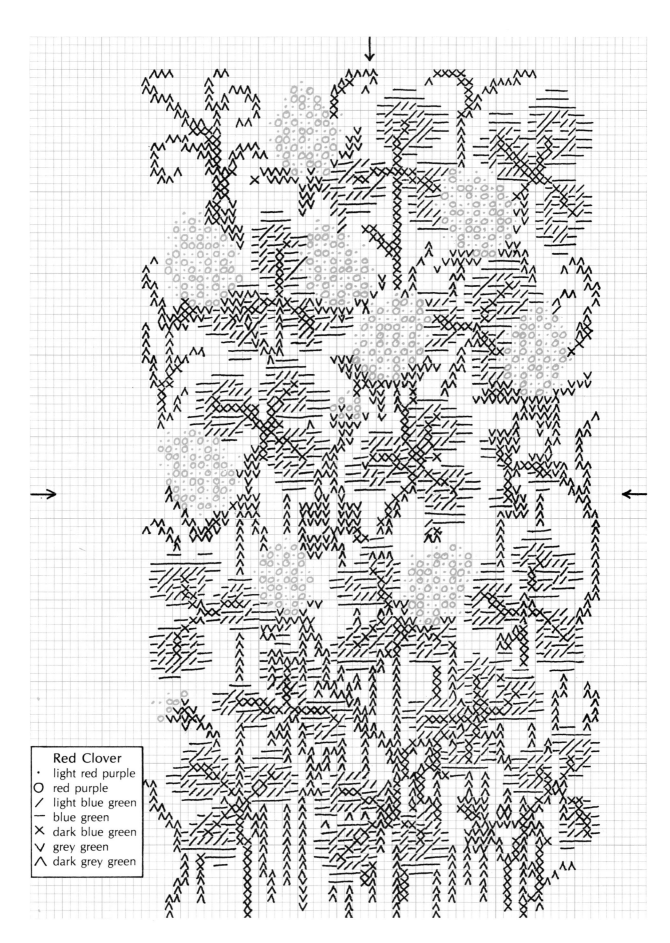

Red Clover
- · light red purple
- O red purple
- / light blue green
- — blue green
- ✕ dark blue green
- V grey green
- ∧ dark grey green

54

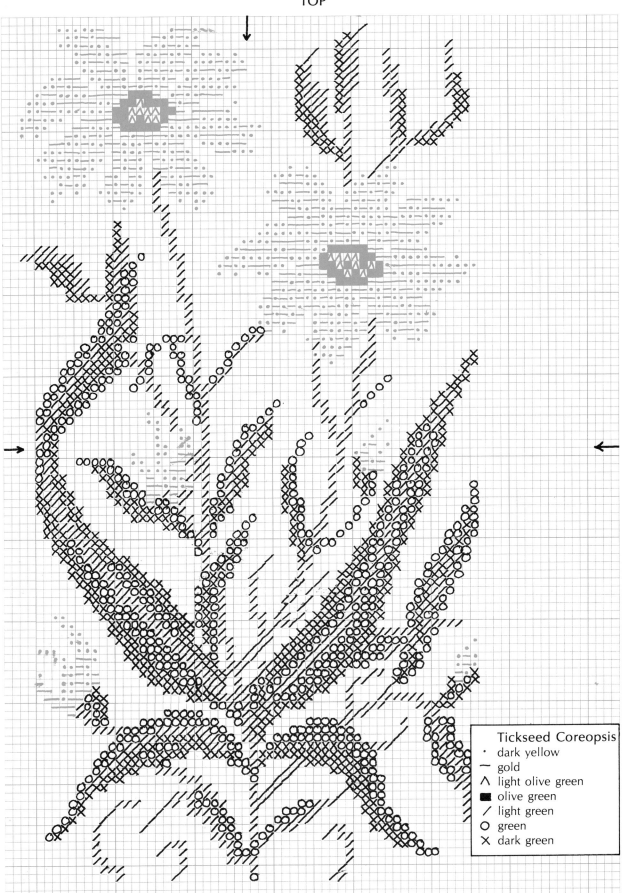

Tickseed Coreopsis
· dark yellow
— gold
∧ light olive green
■ olive green
╱ light green
○ green
╳ dark green

TOP

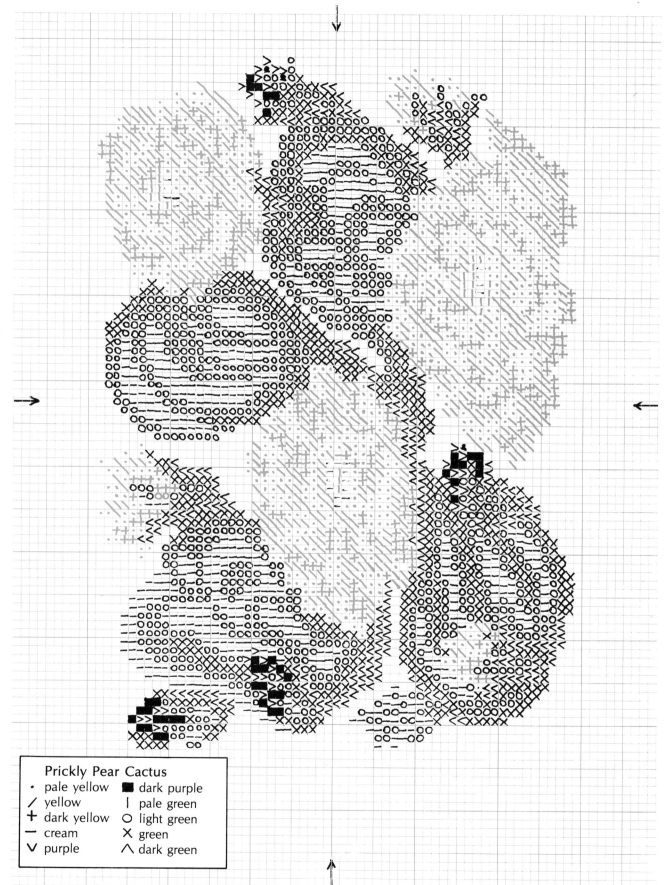

Prickly Pear Cactus

- · pale yellow   ■ dark purple
- / yellow | pale green
- + dark yellow   O light green
- − cream   X green
- V purple   ∧ dark green

56

TOP

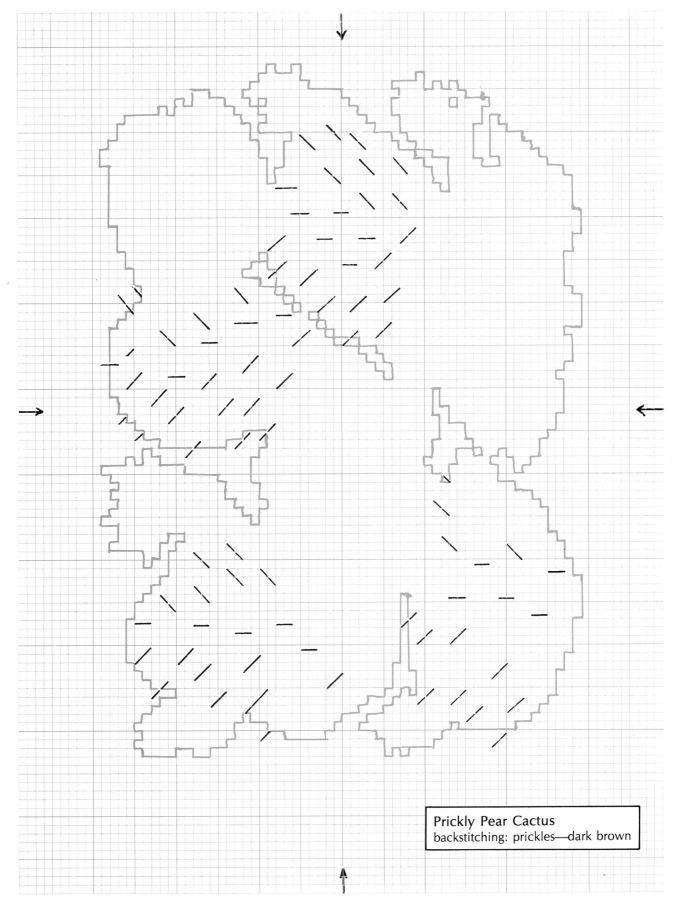

Prickly Pear Cactus
backstitching: prickles—dark brown

57

Wild Man of the Earth
- · white
- ∧ pale rose
- O rose
- X dark rose
- ■ dark green
- / light yellow green
- \ light green
- V green
- I pale green
- + yellow green

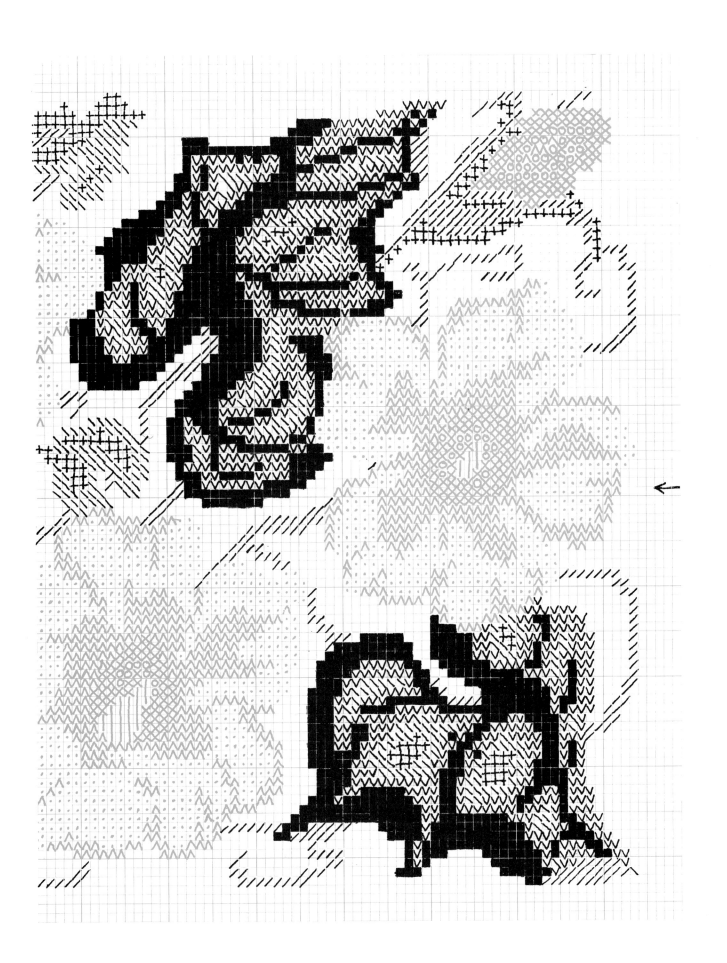

Yellow Jessamine
- · light yellow
- \ yellow
- + dark yellow
- | light rust
- O pale green
- < light green
- ✕ green
- ■ dark green
- — yellow green

Purple Joe-Pye Weed
X purple
• light purple
/ light green
— green
+ dark green
V light olive green
\ olive green

Indian Strawberry
- · yellow
- V dark yellow
- + red
- ∧ dark red
- / light yellow green
- ○ yellow green
- − dark yellow green
- | light green
- × green
- \ dark green

TOP

Wild Azalea
× dark peach
O peach
· light peach
■ brown
V light yellow green
/ yellow green
+ dark yellow green
\ light green
I green

TOP

Wild Azalea
backstitching: dark peach

65

TOP

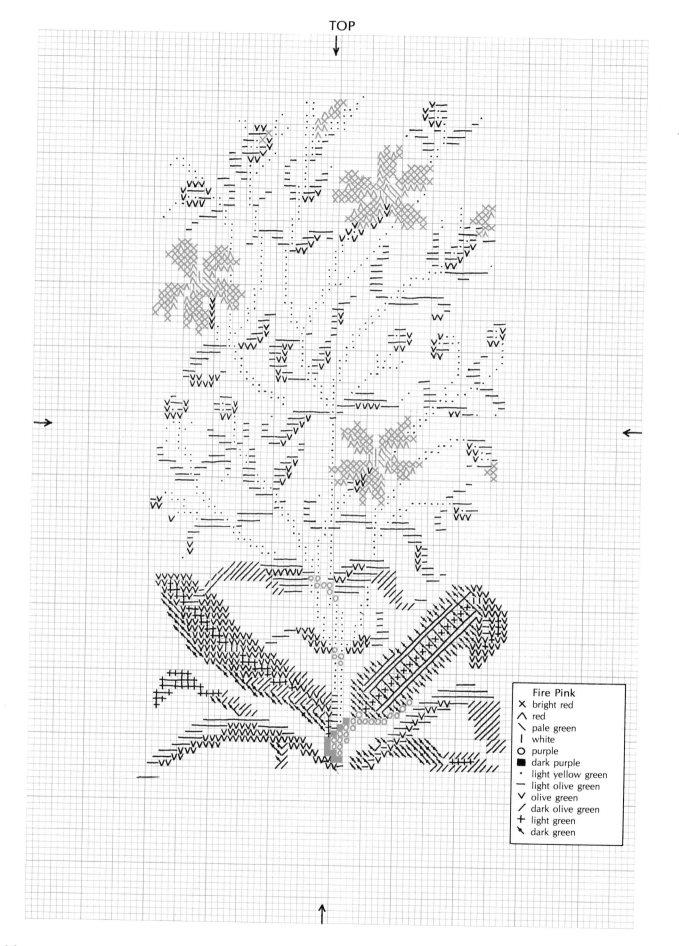

Fire Pink
- ✗ bright red
- ∧ red
- ╲ pale green
- | white
- ○ purple
- ■ dark purple
- · light yellow green
- — light olive green
- ∨ olive green
- ╱ dark olive green
- + light green
- ⋎ dark green

66

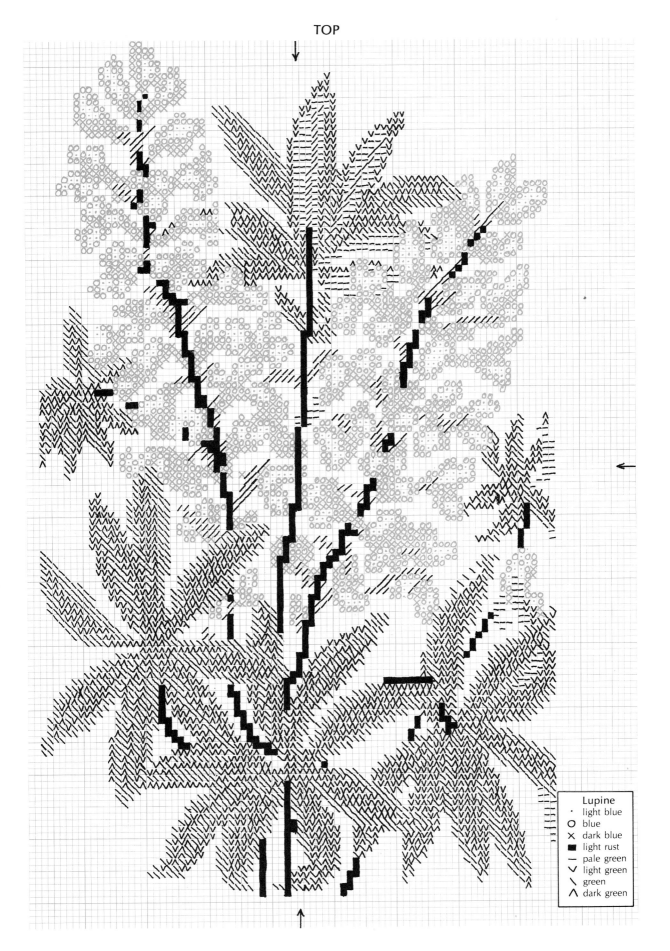

Lupine
· light blue
O blue
X dark blue
■ light rust
— pale green
V light green
\ green
Λ dark green

Carolina Pink

\ light rose	— light olive green	| yellow green	V grey green
O rose	∧ light yellow green	/ light grey green	X dark grey green
■ dark rose			

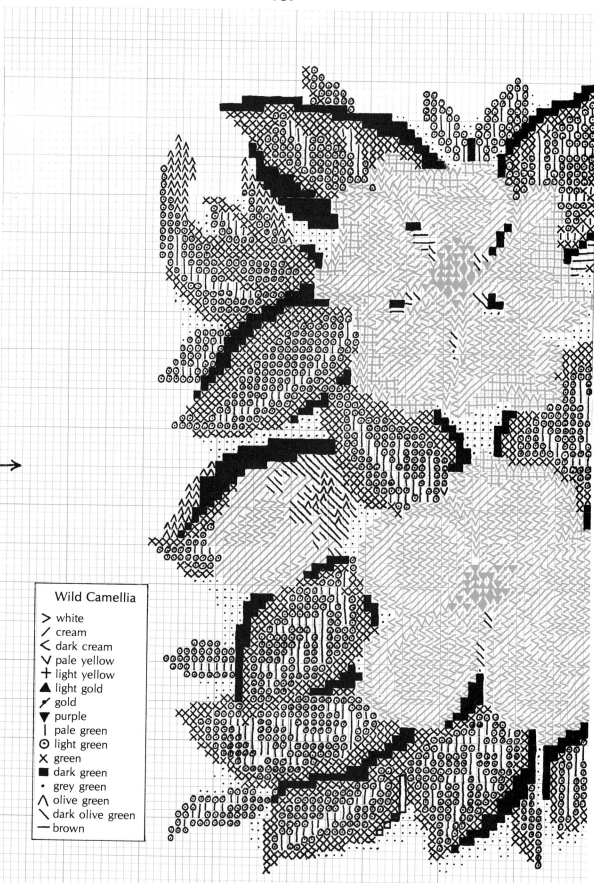

Wild Camellia

> white
/ cream
< dark cream
V pale yellow
+ light yellow
▲ light gold
✔ gold
▼ purple
| pale green
⊙ light green
X green
■ dark green
• grey green
∧ olive green
\ dark olive green
— brown

70

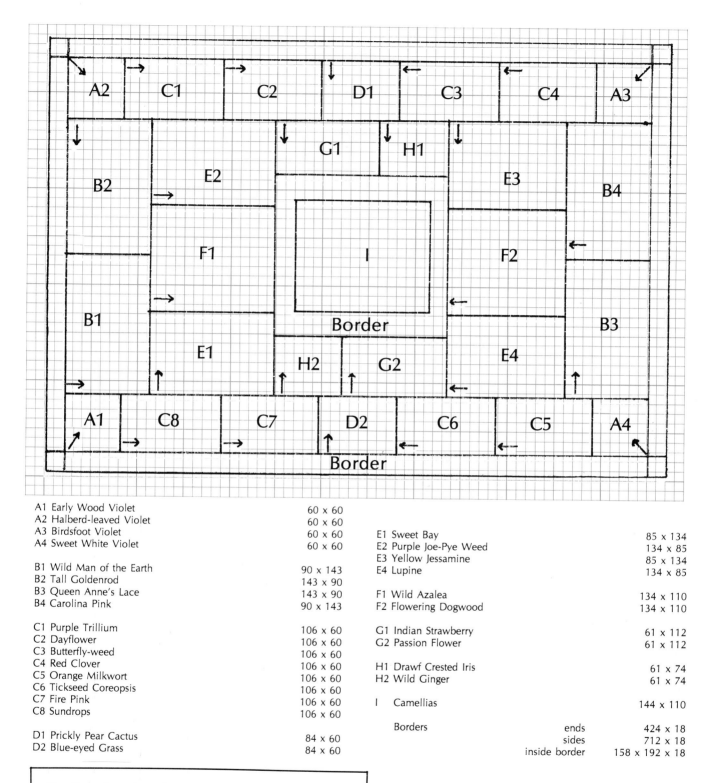

A1 Early Wood Violet	60 x 60			
A2 Halberd-leaved Violet	60 x 60			
A3 Birdsfoot Violet	60 x 60	E1 Sweet Bay	85 x 134	
A4 Sweet White Violet	60 x 60	E2 Purple Joe-Pye Weed	134 x 85	
		E3 Yellow Jessamine	85 x 134	
B1 Wild Man of the Earth	90 x 143	E4 Lupine	134 x 85	
B2 Tall Goldenrod	143 x 90			
B3 Queen Anne's Lace	143 x 90	F1 Wild Azalea	134 x 110	
B4 Carolina Pink	90 x 143	F2 Flowering Dogwood	134 x 110	
C1 Purple Trillium	106 x 60	G1 Indian Strawberry	61 x 112	
C2 Dayflower	106 x 60	G2 Passion Flower	61 x 112	
C3 Butterfly-weed	106 x 60			
C4 Red Clover	106 x 60	H1 Drawf Crested Iris	61 x 74	
C5 Orange Milkwort	106 x 60	H2 Wild Ginger	61 x 74	
C6 Tickseed Coreopsis	106 x 60			
C7 Fire Pink	106 x 60	I Camellias	144 x 110	
C8 Sundrops	106 x 60			

A1 Early Wood Violet   60 x 60
A2 Halberd-leaved Violet   60 x 60
A3 Birdsfoot Violet   60 x 60   E1 Sweet Bay   85 x 134
A4 Sweet White Violet   60 x 60   E2 Purple Joe-Pye Weed   134 x 85
                                               E3 Yellow Jessamine   85 x 134
B1 Wild Man of the Earth   90 x 143   E4 Lupine   134 x 85
B2 Tall Goldenrod   143 x 90
B3 Queen Anne's Lace   143 x 90   F1 Wild Azalea   134 x 110
B4 Carolina Pink   90 x 143   F2 Flowering Dogwood   134 x 110

C1 Purple Trillium   106 x 60   G1 Indian Strawberry   61 x 112
C2 Dayflower   106 x 60   G2 Passion Flower   61 x 112
C3 Butterfly-weed   106 x 60
C4 Red Clover   106 x 60   H1 Drawf Crested Iris   61 x 74
C5 Orange Milkwort   106 x 60   H2 Wild Ginger   61 x 74
C6 Tickseed Coreopsis   106 x 60
C7 Fire Pink   106 x 60   I Camellias   144 x 110
C8 Sundrops   106 x 60

                                                  Borders   ends   424 x 18
D1 Prickly Pear Cactus   84 x 60   sides   712 x 18
D2 Blue-eyed Grass   84 x 60   inside border   158 x 192 x 18

The dimensions given above represent the number of threads of the stitched area for each of the wildflower designs. To allow for assembling the designs into a rug, add 18 threads to each dimension — 3 threads for the binding stitch and rows of continental stitches, and 15 threads (1½" of canvas) for seam allowance.

72

Making a Rug

The wildflower designs in this book can be set together to make a spectacular needlepoint rug. You might decide to make the rug gradually by yourself, or you could tempt your civic or church group to undertake the project as a fund raising effort, the final rug to be auctioned or raffled off for a worthy cause.

The decision to use the patterns in a rug should be made *before* you start stitching any of the designs because they must be done uniformly with special considerations as to background colors and size of each wildflower piece. *You must plan your rug in advance to know which direction to stitch each design so that all of the stitches in the finished rug will be going in the same direction.*

The diagram shown on the facing page illustrates one way in which the different-sized wildflower designs will fit into a rug. The border design shown on the following page may be used around the outside of the rug. (Notice the interesting corner detail.) An inside border was also used to frame the central piece.

For a rug measuring approximately 6 x 4 feet (712 x 472 stitches), each of the 29 wildflower designs and the border design on page 74 should be worked on 10 mesh mono canvas and carefully blocked. (See Blocking Needlework.) The list given indicates the finished dimensions of each design. *To each of these dimensions, add a total of 18 more threads to allow for the seam allowance and the binding and continental stitches necessary in assembling your rug.*

Following the rug diagram, arrange the blocked finished pieces with the top of each design facing in the direction indicated by the arrow. Notice that the rug is designed so that it can be viewed from any angle without being "upside down."

With right sides together, align the threads of adjoining designs and hand-stitch the pieces together with carpet thread, using a backstitch and going through each hole in the canvases. Fifteen threads are allowed for the seam allowance. On the right side, be sure you have left three additional threads on either side of the seam exposed (for a total of six "bare" threads).

Open the canvas seams on the back side of the rug. Work over the center two threads (one on either side of the seam) with one row of binding stitch (see diagram). Work the binding stitch through the top canvas and the seam allowance on the back side of the rug.

Work two rows of the continental stitch on either side of the binding stitch. Do not work these four rows of continental through the seam allowance on the back of the rug or the finished rug will pucker.

Join the borders to the rug with the same technique of binding stitch with two rows of continental on either side. Work two rows of binding stitches over four threads all around the outside border of the finished rug.

Even though the individual pieces were blocked before being sewn together, the finished rug will need to be blocked also. To finish the binding process, lay the blocked rug right side up on a flat surface. Pin rug-binding tape ¼ inch beyond the worked area along the outside edges of the rug, starting and ending the tape at the midpoint of one side and overlapping the ends 1 inch. Miter the corners as you come to them.

Stitch the rug-binding tape to the canvas hem allowance just beyond the worked area either by hand (backstitch) with carpet thread, or by machine. Trim the canvas mesh seam allowance ¼ inch narrower than the binding tape, taking care not to cut into the tape itself. Trim the corners of the canvas (not the tape) diagonally. Apply a little white glue around the edges of the canvas to keep them from ravelling.

Fold the canvas hem allowances against the rug and pin. Whip the inner edges and mitered corners of the raw canvas to the back of the rug and remove the pins.

Turn the binding to the wrong side and, folding one side of the rug at a time, pin to the back of the rug. Hemstitch the unattached edges of the binding to the back of the rug and slipstitch the mitered corners. Remove the pins. If you wish, line the back of the rug for added protection.

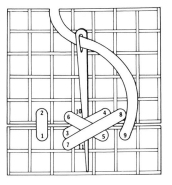

Binding stitch: Bring the needle up on the odd numbers and down on the even numbers.

Border
- · light green
- ✕ dark green
- O orange or other color
  background: light blue grey

74

Working from a Charted Design

Please note that the words graph and chart are used interchangeably. They mean the same thing. The most important thing to remember in working with a charted design is that each square on the graph represents one stitch.

To determine the size of a finished piece that will be worked by following a graph, count the squares in the height and width of the design. All of the charts in this book have been drawn on graph paper with 10 squares to the inch, with every fifth intersection line darker. (Some have been reduced to fit on the page.) No matter how many squares there are in an inch on the graph, the design can be stitched on a canvas or fabric of any mesh you choose. (Mesh is the number of stitches allowed for in an inch of fabric or canvas.) A design charted on 10 squares-to-the-inch graph paper may be stitched on 12 mesh needlepoint canvas, 22 mesh hardanger cloth, 14 mesh Aida cloth, 5 mesh quick point canvas, or any other mesh canvas or cloth that you want to use. The fact that the chart shows 10 squares in an inch does not affect the size of the finished work; the number of stitches that you work in an inch determines the finished size.

Mathematics can be irritating when you are anxious to begin stitching, but it is necessary. If you do not figure carefully at the outset, you may find that you have bought much more material than you need, or much worse, that your stitches run off the edge of the material. In this case, the whole piece will have to be discarded and begun again. Here is a useful formula:

Number of squares in the height of the charted design
divided by
number of stitches in an inch of your needlework
equals
number of inches high the stitched design will be.

The same formula works for determining the width.

When you know how long and how wide your stitched design will be, you must then allow extra material around the edges for whatever you wish for background, plus 1 to 1½ inches all around for finishing.

Example: A charted design counts 106 squares high by 60 squares wide. To work the design in needlepoint on 10 mesh canvas, divide 106 by 10 and 60 by 10. The design will work out to be 10.6 (rounded to 11) inches high and 6 inches wide. If you want an additional 1 inch of background stitches all around the design, then the finished piece will measure 13 by 8 inches. Add 1½ inches of canvas all around for finishing, and you will need a piece of 10 mesh canvas that measures 16 by 11 inches.

To work the same design in cross stitch on 14 mesh Aida cloth, divide 106 by 14 and 60 by 14. Your design will work out to be 7.57 inches high and 4.29 inches wide. Round off the figures to 8 by 4½ inches. If you want an additional ½ inch all around of background material, the finished piece will measure approximately 9 by 5½ inches. Add 1½ inches all around the design for finishing, and you know you will need a piece of Aida cloth that measures 12 by 8½ inches.

To begin stitching from a charted design, remember that one square on the graph paper represents one stitch. If you have never worked from a chart, your first look at so many small squares of different colors or color symbols may discourage you. But, if you can see to do needlework, you can see well enough to follow a chart.

There are, however, ways to make counting the squares in the chart easier. A stitch finder is used with the chart; it has metal strips that you line up underneath the row of squares you are counting. If you do not purchase a stitch finder, you can use a strip of poster paper in the same way. A standing clear plastic book holder is also an asset, as your angle of vision on a chart is much better when the chart is upright than when it is lying down.

Some experienced needleworkers help themselves count on a color-coded chart by marking lightly with a pencil those squares they have worked. When the needlework is finished, the pencil markings can be erased so that the chart may be used again.

Charts can be either solid colored, color coded, or both. There are advantages to each type of chart. A colored chart will give you a much better idea of how the finished piece will look, but it is sometimes difficult to see the lines of the chart. Color coded charts, such as those appearing in this book, have a symbol to represent each color in the design. If the color code indicates that the symbol x stands for gold, make a gold stitch for each x on the chart. To aid in reading the charts in this book, each design is done in two colors, black and blue. The blue areas represent the actual wildflower blossom while the black areas stand for the foliage. Each symbol represents only one color of yarn on each chart, but may differ from one chart to the next because color schemes for the wildflowers differ.

Work from the center out. Begin counting at the center of the chart and stitching at the center of the material. Usually it is easier to work up from the center and complete the upper part of the design, then finish the lower part. However, it may be easier to outline a central figure, beginning with, or close to, the center stitch, then work to fill in the upper portions of the design, followed by the lower portions.

Find the middle of the chart by counting the number of squares up the height and the number of squares across the width. (These dimensions are given on the Key on each chart.) The place at which the exact center of these lines cross each other is the center of the chart. Mark this center point on the chart.

Find the center of your canvas or cloth by folding it in half lengthwise, then again crosswise (Figure 1). Mark the center. The safest method is with a sewing thread that can be snipped out after the work is begun. If you use a pencil, use it lightly. Never use a felt-tipped marker because it will bleed through the needlework.

The center of the chart may fall on one square of the design, or it may be somewhere in the background stitches. The center of the chart is not the same as the center of the design. See the following examples (Figures 2, 3, 4) for how to start working a design from the center.

After the first stitch, work stitches to the right, left, or up, counting squares on the chart that are the same color and working the same number of squares in the same places on the canvas or cloth.

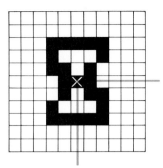

Figure 2. If the center of the chart is one square, begin by making that stitch.

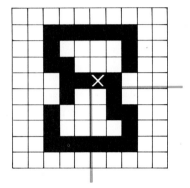

Figure 3. If the center is a point where four stitches meet, choose either of the upper two squares and begin stitching.

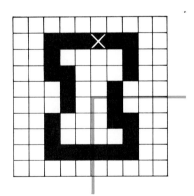

Figure 4. If the center of the chart falls on the background, count up to the nearest design square and begin stitching there.

Figure 1. Find the center of material by folding it in half lengthwise, then crosswise.

Working Cross Stitch and Needlepoint

In cross stitch, each under stitch of the cross should slant in the same direction, and the crossing upper stitch should slant consistently in the opposite direction. You may work all of the under stitches first, then go back and cross each (Figures 5a and 5b), or you may complete each cross stitch before beginning the next (Figure 6).

For needlepoint projects, use a tent stitch to work the design and a stitch of your choice to fill in the background. A tent stitch is any stitch which covers one thread intersection on top of the canvas and two thread intersections underneath: there are several versions of the tent stitch. Sometimes, it is necessary to change direction with your stitching; for example, you may need to change from working from left to right to working down. A half cross stitch will allow this to be accomplished. A half cross stitch in needlepoint covers one thread intersection on top of the canvas and only one thread intersection underneath. See the blue stitches in Figure 7 for examples.

When possible, in an area of many stitches of the same color, use the diagonal tent stitch, also known as the basketweave (Figure 8). This stitch is one of the strongest of the tent stitches and distorts the canvas less than most other stitches as it is worked.

A suggestion for a background stitch is the diagonal mosaic stitch. It fits in particularly well with the slant of the tent stitch, and speeds up boring background work (Figure 9).

Backstitching or topstitching, is indicated on a separate graph by lines. Finish the cross stitches or needlepoint stitches before working the backstitching. Use less yarn for backstitching on needlepoint by separating yarn strands, or use a full strand of embroidery floss. Backstitches may run along the sides, above, below, or diagonally across needlepoint and cross stitch stitches. They should be made by a "punch and stab" motion, not by "needle-through" (Figure 10).

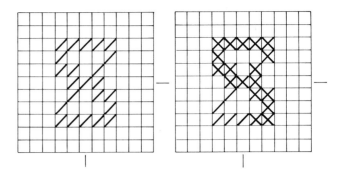

Figures 5a & 5b. Work all the stitches for the under stitch of the cross stitch in one direction; then make the upper stitch in the opposite direction.

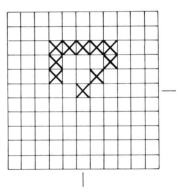

Figure 6. Or, work each cross stitch completely as you go.

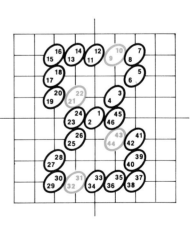

Figure 7. To follow any stitch diagram, bring the needle up from underneath the canvas on odd numbers, (1, 3, 5) and put the needle through from above on even numbers (2, 4, 6). Blue stitches indicate half cross stitches.

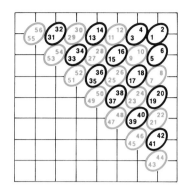

Figure 8. The diagonal tent stitch, also called the basketweave, should be used for backgrounds and any design areas that have many stitches of the same color. After the first three stitches, the rows drawn in black are worked diagonally down, with the needle put through the canvas vertically. Rows of stitches drawn in blue are to be worked diagonally up, putting the needle through the canvas horizontally. Remember that the needle comes up from underneath the canvas on the odd numbers and goes in from the front on the even numbers.

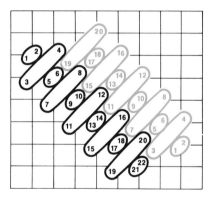

Figure 9. Follow the numbers for stitching the diagonal mosaic stitch.

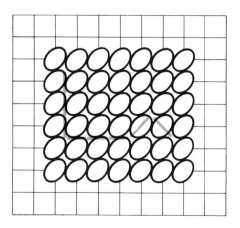

Figure 10. Embroidery stitches such as topstitching or backstitching are worked after needlepoint is completed.

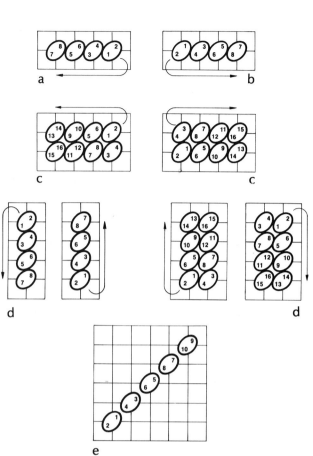

Figure 11. (a) This tent stitch is called the continental stitch. (b) If you must work from left to right, use a "stick and stab" rather than "needle through" method. Make sure each row of stitches slants in the same direction. (c) Two rows can be worked at once. (d) Illustrated also is how to work the tent stitch vertically, in single and double rows. (e) To work a single row of tent stitches slanting from lower left to upper right, use a "stick and stab" motion, not "needle through."

Blocking Needlework

The purpose of blocking is to pull the threads of the canvas or fabric on which the needlework was done back "on grain." Blocking can make up for a multitude of mistakes made while working the piece, but it cannot correct entirely a piece that has been worked so tightly that the canvas is stretched permanently out of shape. The moral is to work with an even, slightly loose tension.

If a needlepoint piece is badly out of shape, it must be soaked in *cold* water. (This step is to be avoided if possible, especially if a painted canvas was used. The colors of the painted canvas may bleed, not because of the paint or ink, most of which is guaranteed not to run, but because of the very necessary sizing which comes loose from the canvas and floats the colors through the piece.) If a piece *must* be soaked, be sure to dry it flat, rather than upright, to give less chance of the colors bleeding onto one another.

Alternative methods for dampening a piece before pinning it to the blocking board are rolling it in a wet towel until the piece is damp or spraying it with water. Steam pressing your work with a wet cloth after the piece is pinned down is usually enough for pieces that are not too distorted, as is often the case with bargello and pieces worked on a frame or hoop.

The steps to be followed in pinning down a needlework piece are always the same except that wet pieces should be blocked right side up and pieces to be steamed should be blocked upside down. (The reason for this is to retain stitch texture and prevent flattening the face of the work.) Pinning may be done on a plywood board, a drawing board, or a cutting board. If the piece is small, the ironing board may be used.

First, mark a square or rectangle the size of the canvas on the board or on paper attached to the board. (If you do a lot of blocking, it will be useful to mark a board in 1-inch squares across the whole surface so that pieces of many different sizes can be blocked on the board.) Aluminum push pins are the best to use for blocking because they are sharp and do not rust. Never, never pin into the worked part of the canvas.

Most needlepoint requiring blocking has become slightly diamond shaped. To correct this, pin your needlepoint to the marked board as follows:

Pin the upper left corner of your piece to the board. Place a pin 1 inch from the corner along the top of the piece and another pin 1 inch from the corner along the side. Repeat the same procedure in the corner diagonally opposite.

Beginning from the upper left corner, pin down the left side of the piece to the bottom left corner, spacing the pins about 1 inch apart. Stop the pins 2 inches from the bottom corner.

Work across the top of the piece in the same manner, stopping the pins about 2 inches from the upper right corner. Repeat down the right side to the bottom right corner. Finally, pin from the bottom left corner to the bottom right. If the piece is soaking wet, allow to dry thoroughly—at least 24 hours. If the piece is face down, use a wet cloth and steam iron until it is damp through and allow to dry thoroughly. Drying is important because the needlepoint will revert to its original warped shape if re-moved from the blocking board while still wet.

Cross stitch and other embroidery work should be blocked on a heavily padded surface, such as can be formed with several layers of toweling. Work with the embroidery face down. Using a steam iron and a light spray starch, press and pull the embroidery to the correct shape with the backs of your hands. Let it dry in the correct shape before moving it.

Choosing Colors and Materials

Every attempt was made to be as accurate as possible in the colors and shapes of the wildflower designs. But don't hesitate to alter the color, particularly the backgrounds, to suit your tastes. It is in the choosing of colors, materials, and use that the needleworker creates an original piece of work from a printed chart. But keep in mind the one rule that will result in an interesting and vibrant product: there must be at least one very dark and at least one very light tone in the colors used. Other color tones may range from dark to medium to light, but without the contrast of a very light and a very dark, the design will be uninteresting.

There are no colors that are "wrong" used together, just as there are no color combinations that are "better" than other color combinations. Any combination of any color, muted and subdued or bright and contrasting, is "right" if you like it.

When selecting the materials that you use for needlework, rely on your past experience and the advice of other needleworkers. Penelope canvas with a woven vertical thread and double horizontal threads is the most durable. Antique (beige) colored canvas is less likely to show canvas through the finished work than white canvas. If you use a mono canvas, which is easier to see than penelope, make sure that it is interlocking. This will insure even stitches. The mono canvas used for bargello stitches is not suitable for needlepoint.

You may use tapestry yarn, spun for needlepoint, or Persian yarn.

There are many materials used for count-thread cross stitch. The only absolute requirement is that the cloth be evenly woven; that is, that there be as many threads in an inch horizontally as there are threads in an inch vertically. The number of threads from a strand of the embroidery floss that you use depends upon the weight of the cloth used.

Bibliography

Batson, Wade T. *Wildflowers in South Carolina*. Columbia: University of South Carolina Press, 1964.

Bruce, Hal. *How to Grow Wildflowers and Wild Shrubs and Trees in Your Own Garden*. New York: Alfred A. Knopf, 1976.

Campbell, Carlos C.; Hutson, William F.; Macon, Hershal L.; and Sharp, Aaron J. *Great Smoky Mountains Wildflowers*. Knoxville: University of Tennessee Press, 1964.

Dana, Mrs. William Starr. *How to Know the Wild Flowers*. New York: Dover Publishing Company, 1963.

Dean, Blanche E. *Trees and Shrubs in the Heart of Dixie*. Southern University Press, 1968.

Dean, Blanche E.; Mason, Amy; and Thomas, Joab L. *Wildflowers of Alabama and Adjoining States*. Tuscaloosa: University of Alabama Press, 1973.

Dormon, Caroline. *Natives Preferred*. Baton Rouge: Claitor's Book Store, 1965.

Fielder, Mildred. *Plant Medicine and Folklore*. New York: Winchester Press, 1975.

Fischer, Helen F., and Harshbarger, Gretchen F. *The Flower Family Album*. New York: The University of Minnesota Press, 1941.

Greene, Wilhelmina F., and Blomquist, Hugo L. *Flowers of the South: Native and Exotic*. Chapel Hill: The University of North Carolina Press, 1953.

Houseman, Ethel H. *The Illustrated Encyclopedia of American Wildflowers*. New York: Garden City Publishing Company, 1947.

Hylander, Clarence J., and Johnston, Edith F. *The MacMillan Wild Flower Book*. New York: The MacMillan Company, 1954.

Klimas, John, and Cunningham, James A. *Wildflowers of Eastern America*. New York: Alfred A. Knopf, 1974.

Peterson, Roger T., and McKenny, Margaret. *A Field Guide to Wildflowers of Northeastern and North-central North America*. Boston: Houghton Mifflin Company, 1968.

Petrides, George A. *A Field Guide to Trees and Shrubs*. Boston: Houghton Mifflin Company, 1958.

Radford, Albert E.; Ahles, Harry E.; and Bell, C. Ritchie. *Manual of the Vascular Flora of the Carolinas*. Chapel Hill: The University of North Carolina Press, 1968.

Rickett, Harold W. *The Odyssey Book of American Wildflowers*. New York: The Odyssey Press, 1964.

Rickett, Harold W. *Wild Flowers of America*. New York: Crown Publishers, 1953.

Stupka, Arthur. *Wildflowers in Color*. New York: Harper & Row, 1965.

Wherry, Edgar T. *Wild Flower Guide: Northeastern and Midland United States*. New York: Doubleday & Company, 1948.

Zim, Herbert S., and Martin, Alexander C. *Flowers: A Guide to Familiar American Wildflowers*. New York: Golden Press, 1950.